AFTER THE END OF HISTORY

After *the* End

of History

CONVERSATIONS WITH

Francis Fukuyama

Edited by

Mathilde Fasting

Georgetown University Press • WASHINGTON, DC

The publisher is not responsible for third-party websites or their content. URL links were active at time of publication.

Library of Congress Cataloging-in-Publication Data

Names: Fukuyama, Francis, interviewee. | Fasting, Mathilde C., interviewer.
Title: After the end of history : conversations with Francis Fukuyama / Mathilde Fasting with Francis Fukuyama.
Description: Washington, DC : Georgetown University Press, 2021. | Includes bibliographical references and index.
Identifiers: LCCN 2020034404 | ISBN 9781647120863 (hardcover) | ISBN 9781647120870 (ebook)
Subjects: LCSH: Fukuyama, Francis—Interviews. | History—Philosophy. | Historians—United States—Interviews. | World politics—1989– | Liberalism. | Civilization, Modern—21st century. | Biotechnology.
Classification: LCC D16.8 .F847 2021 | DDC 901—dc23
LC record available at https://lccn.loc.gov/2020034404

⊚ This paper meets the requirements of ANSI/NISO Z39.48-1992 (Permanence of Paper).

22 21   9 8 7 6 5 4 3 2 First printing

Printed in the United States of America

Cover design by Amanda Hudson, Faceout Studio
Cover art by Kjell Torriset, photographed by Hans Kristian Thorbjørnsen
Interior design by Classic City Composition

Contents

Editor's Preface

I would not have thought it necessary to defend democracy and its underlying values in 2021, more than thirty years after the fall of the Berlin Wall. Although the decades after World War II saw many conflicts, such as the Vietnam War and the Balkan conflicts of the 1990s, the period has largely been characterized by peace and prosperity and a globalization that has brought millions of people out of poverty. In light of these developments, it was hard to imagine that recession, military expansion, social unrest, and fear would once again dominate global politics. In the last few years, however, postwar optimism has been turned on its head. Whether we have reason to fear where this is going or whether current authoritarian tendencies and nationalistic protectionism will turn out to be fleeting phenomena depends on the strength of our democracies. Are they capable of handling the challenges they currently face, and, if not, how can we make them more resilient? One thing seems certain: in a world where an increasing number of political tasks require complex and often internationally coordinated responses, the last thing we need is nationalist protectionism and weak democracies.

One of the thinkers currently grappling with these questions is the political scientist Francis Fukuyama. Many know Fukuyama as the person who proclaimed liberal democracy's victory after the fall of the wall to mark the "end of history." In 2019 it was thirty years since the essay "The End of History?" was published in the small journal *The National Interest*. The book *The End of History and the Last Man* followed a few years later, in 1992, sealing Fukuyama's fame. The "end of history" term will, it seems, forever be tied to his name.

Few public intellectuals have been more influential and prolific than Fukuyama. There was no end of history for him: he has kept on writing for more than thirty years, presenting deep insights into the workings of political order, its perils and challenges, and the importance of institutions for well-functioning states. His alternative approach to human cooperation evolved slowly in his mind, and in his work, until it found its final expression in *The Origins of Political Order: From Prehuman Times to the French Revolution* in 2011. This bio-anthropological approach breaks with classical liberal theory and shines an explanatory light on the problems and decay of some contemporary democracies.

Fukuyama has observed weaknesses in Western political development for a long time, especially since the financial crisis in 2008. In *Political Order and Political Decay: From the Industrial Revolution to the Globalization of Democracy* (2014), he points out that several conditions represent threats to the functioning of liberal democracy. He expands on his worries in *Identity: The Demand for Dignity and the Politics of Resentment* (2018), expressing a deep concern for the current growth of populist movements and more authoritarian political leaders in the United States and across the West more generally. His life's work reveals what we need to address the contemporary issues of populist leaders, poor understanding of democracy's underpinnings, and rapid technological change. Further, he strongly argues for the importance of having a well-functioning government when crisis hits.

The idea of this project was originally born almost ten years ago. My first encounter with Fukuyama was through his book *The Origins of Political Order*. What caught my interest was his explanation of the historical roots of liberal democracy. Being Norwegian, I asked myself why an American political thinker showed such interest in Scandinavia and Denmark, in particular. Which part of these countries' histories made Fukuyama point to them as ideals of political order? When I read *Political Order and Political Decay* three years later, it struck me how fragile the balance of power and institutions in liberal democracies are.

My first idea was to explain his thought to a Norwegian audience and relate his ideas specifically to challenges facing Norwegian society. However, after meeting and talking to Fukuyama in 2018, the idea of a dialogue emerged as the best way to express Fukuyama's important insights in a way that could also highlight the scope and variety of his work over more than three decades. A key element in Fukuyama's thought is found in Plato's dialogues, and so the dialogue seems especially appropriate when trying to explore the richness of Fukuyama's many books and articles. My hope is that through this dialogue, Fukuyama will emerge as an engaged conversation partner for the reader and not a distant, intellectual political thinker.

After I first met Fukuyama in Oslo in 2018, I was fortunate to get the chance to read the manuscript of *Identity*. This made it clear to me how consistently he has pursued the idea of recognition that first appeared in *The End of History*. A year later, over a few days in March 2019, I met with Fukuyama to interview him about his ideas in more detail. We met in his office at Stanford, among all his books.

In February 2020 we met again over three days in Oslo. During this time, we had the opportunity to elaborate on observations Fukuyama had made in his many talks and discussions after the publication of his book *Identity* and in commemoration of the thirtieth anniversary of the fall of the Berlin Wall in November 2019. The interviews, as they appear in this book, have been edited for the sake of clarity and to eliminate some repetition.

ONE

What Has Happened
after the End of History?

I n the current political context, there are many dark clouds. The
question is whether liberal democracies will prove themselves capable in rainy days. The 2016 election of Donald Trump, Brexit, and
the rise of populism in Europe are contributing to a more unstable and
uncertain future, and the rise of China is altering the global balance
of power. How does this influence liberal democracies?

Liberal Democracies Are Taken for Granted

**We have in the West been taking liberal democracy more or less for granted
for the past fifty years. What has happened after the end of history? Why do
we need this conversation now?**

I think you are right. In the United States nobody has really felt
threatened. The basic constitutional system has worked for a very long
time. Richard Nixon challenged it, and that led to his resignation
and the whole Watergate scandal, but, in a sense, I don't think that
the threat he posed to the system was nearly as great as the one that
Donald Trump poses. Nixon never openly tried to undermine his own
Justice Department or the FBI. He denied that he was guilty of the
things that he was accused of. He lied about things, but he didn't say
the whole effort to hold the president accountable was a big hoax or
a big fraud. With Trump it is different, and I think that this kind of
disrespect for legal and constitutional institutions is really spreading
to too many parts of the world. He likes to attack existing institutions.
And I think this is a very dangerous tendency.

In your books about political order, you have talked about the "miracle of modern liberal democracy, in which strong states capable of enforcing law are nonetheless checked by law and by legislatures, finding a balance of power that made no one dominant and forcing all to compromise."[1] People living in liberal democracies will have a sense of what they are, but it is useful to repeat and clarify. Let us start by defining liberal democracies: what are they?

Well, in my view a liberal democracy is three separate institutions. One of them is a modern state, meaning a state that is capable of actually delivering services and protecting the country both internally and externally. The second institution is a rule of law that limits the power of the state so that the state only behaves lawfully according to rules that are agreed upon by the community. The third set of institutions are the ones of democratic accountability that make sure that the state reflects the interests of the whole people.

Ultimately, an important part of liberal democracy is a combination of liberal institutions that limit power and treat citizens fairly and democratic ones that respond to the will of the population. Those two are not necessarily aligned with one another. The other thing that's very difficult to achieve is balance because, on the one hand, you want a state that is strong enough to be able to actually do things—to enforce laws and arrest criminals and so forth—but, on the other hand, you don't want it to be so strong that it violates the rights of its citizens. And somehow you have to have both a strong state that can constrain and at the same time let people lead their lives. This balance is important.

You are preoccupied with the value of the modern state. Why?

Liberal democracies are also modern states capable of delivering services, rules of law that limit the power of the state, and democratically accountable institutions. Of those, democracy is the easiest to achieve. It is not that difficult to hold elections and get a sense of what the people want. A modern, impersonal state and the rule of law are much more difficult to create. What I think is incredibly common all over the world is a state that delivers services only to people who are supporters of a particular political leader. In other words, the state is not impersonal; it's full of patronage, and corruption sometimes reaches grotesque levels. Sometimes it's captured by military gangs, by families, or by other people, and the state simply ceases functioning. The state is becoming personal instead of being impersonal. I think the impersonality part is really difficult to achieve. A modern state does not treat individuals differently depending on whether you're a friend of the ruler or a relative or something of that sort. Impersonality is something that many countries fail to achieve. This is the argument I tried to make in my two books about political order: that it's hard to achieve because it's not very natural. Your natural instinct is to favor your friends and family, so it's not surprising that corruption keeps coming back. That's why I think that the modern state is fragile. It is a miracle, and it is fragile.

Why is it a miracle?

I think that a modern democracy is a balancing act. On the one hand, you have to have a state. A state is all about power. It's an institution that aggregates and concentrates power and allows the state to enforce laws to defend the community against outsiders to police behavior on the inside. But once you create this powerful state, you need to constrain it, and we do that through the rule of law and also through democracy, which makes the state obedient to the wishes of at least a good proportion of the population. Having that balance is something that's very hard to achieve. Some societies suffer from having no state or a weak state, and others suffer from having an excessively strong state. To get that balance I do think is a bit of a political miracle because we are usually preferring to be friends with our friends, and then not so good friends with people further away from us.

If we keep it on this philosophical level, John Stuart Mill argued that there is an inherent controversy in liberalism between freedom and equality. When freedom increases in society, equality diminishes. You have written the following: "The major arguments concern not the principles of liberal society, but the precise point at which the proper trade-off between liberty and equality should come."[2] Is this true, or does freedom also enhance equality?

I think it is a trade-off, which a lot of people don't want to accept. If you have more liberty, the fact that people have different resources and that they are born with different talents and social endowments means they're not going to end up equal in terms of outcomes. Some people are going to be rich, and some people are not going to succeed, and I think that in order to correct that and equalize outcomes, you need to restrict people's liberty. We've been bouncing back and forth for the last several decades between free markets and attempts to de-regulate the market and the imposition of redistributive policies to make outcomes more equal. But more redistributive policies create a need for a strong state, which in turn restricts people's liberties, and then we react against that restriction. And so we go back to liberaliz-ing everything to increase individual freedom again.

It's kind of a pendulum?

Yes, we don't ever seem to be able to get to a point of stability where we have the right trade-off. Right now I think that we're paying for the excesses of liberty from the 1980s and '90s. This period began with US president Ronald Reagan and British prime minister Margaret Thatcher in the 1980s when they said the state has gotten too big, and it's in the way of economic growth. We liberalized things, including all these banks, which then led to the financial crisis and to greater inequality. It's hard to know when to stop. Now, with the COVID-19 crisis, we're moving rapidly in the other direction, toward stronger executive authority and more restrictions on individual freedom. It's hard not to overshoot on these pendulum swings because once the political pressure builds to move in the opposite direction, politicians seek to outbid one another in how far and fast to move.

A basic question I want to ask is about your important and somewhat new contributions to political theory, especially to democratic theory. You seem to criticize the old liberal contract theories and replace them with your own sociobiological-anchored argument based on a theory of human nature. Is the social human being the basis for your understanding of democracies?

Well, I think that it's not such a new approach. A lot of liberal the-ory is based on an economic view of human beings where you have isolated individuals who have their own preferences and their reason. Essentially, society is just an aggregation of all these individuals. In Europe this theory never caught on to the extent that it did in the

Anglo-Saxon world, but it certainly dominated a lot of American so-cial science thinking about how politics works. I think that's not a cor-rect view of human nature. I believe that there is an innate social side of human behavior that's reflected in, for example, the importance people attach to social recognition. They want other people to recog-nize a kind of inner worth that they have, and they get very angry if that doesn't happen. This desire for recognition explains a lot of mod-ern politics. In that sense, yes, I ground my view of political behavior in a different view of human nature.

The Number of Democracies Has Declined

Freedom House annually reports the number of democracies in the world. This number increased substantially since World War II up un-til 2005. Since then the numbers have slightly decreased. The 2019 Freedom House index shows eighty-seven countries classified as free, and the Freedom of the World Report stated that 2019 was "the 13th consecutive year of decline in global freedom."[3] When Fukuyama pub-lished *The End of History and the Last Man* just after the end of the Cold War, optimism and the number of democracies were peaking. The key to freedom was democracy. We are talking about liberal democracies, a term that consists of two words, "liberal" and "democracy."

How would you best describe a modern understanding of democracy?

There are a couple of ways of approaching that question. A lot of po-litical scientists just give it a procedural definition. They say that de-mocracy has to be free and to have fair, periodic multiparty elections. That's one way of thinking about it. But you can also think about de-mocracy in substantive terms, not just these procedures, but whether the outcomes actually reflect the will of the people. That's where a lot of modern democracies run into trouble because even though you have formally correct procedures, you still don't get to outcomes that people like very much. Why that's the case varies from country to country, but that's one of the problems right now. Then people are blaming democracy for not being what they thought it was, and, well, sometimes they're right. Sometimes elites can game the system in such a way that they really make the system not responsive to the people's true wishes, and that's the problem with lobbying and big interest groups and this sort of thing.

Are you worried?

In terms of global democracy, things obviously look much more pessimistic today than they did thirty years ago in November 1989. We were in the middle of what Samuel Huntington, the great political scientist, labeled the third wave of democratization.[4] The number of democracies increased around the world from about 35 in the year 1972 to over 110, or 115, by the early 2000s. And 1989 was right in the middle of that process. I wrote my essay "The End of History?" shortly before the fall of the Berlin Wall. It came out in the summer of 1989. Obviously that event marked a big jump in the number of democracies as former communist states of Eastern Europe democratized and the former Soviet Union collapsed.

Since the mid-2000s we are in what my colleague Larry Diamond calls a democratic recession.[5] There's been a decline in the number of democracies. Russia and China are now consolidated authoritarian states that are projecting their influence around the world, and you've had the rise of populist movements within established democracies. Populism is perhaps the biggest surprise in this period and has harmed the quality of democracy even in the most established democratic countries, including the United States and Britain.

Is what we are witnessing "temporary counterwaves," to quote Samuel Huntington, or are they fundamental reversals that belie the optimism before the millennium?

I don't think you can answer that at this point. My hope and my suspicion are that they're not permanent, that this doesn't represent the permanent undermining of democracy. But how far it's going to go before it exhausts itself is very hard to say.

I have recently read a very gloomy book that said that what happened after 1989 was not the end of history but "the light that failed."[6] The authors show why liberal democracy in Poland, Hungary, and Russia took a different path after 1989. What are your thoughts about this?

I think that Ivan Krastev and Steve Holmes have a very interesting thesis, which could well be correct. Liberalism as opposed to democracy never really took root in Eastern Europe. In Poland you had an initial elite that was very oriented toward Europe and toward the West. This elite dominated the politics of the first decade after the fall of the Berlin Wall, but there were populist forces that never really accepted the liberal part of liberal democracy. They wanted democratic elections and majority rule, but they didn't accept the idea that a modern society needed to tolerate diversity and that it needed to respect the rule of law. What you're seeing now after thirty years is the erosion of those institutions. Krastev and Holmes also speak about the ongoing demographic crisis in Eastern Europe, which I think has not been adequately recognized. Essentially, a large part of Eastern Europe has emptied out into Western Europe as people seek better opportunities, jobs, and so forth, and that's led to this sense of crisis, both for Hungary and Poland, and other countries in that region.

The authors also mention Russia, saying that it took a different path. Putin's game is to mock liberal democracy. He is holding up a mirror and saying, "What I'm doing to you is just what you are doing to us." The authors claim that the Russians never believed in liberal democracy, they were just forging and faking it, pretending for a while. Russia's ultimate goal is not conversion or assimilation, but revenge and vindication. Is this a valid assumption?

Russia has been trying to find a role for itself, not as part of the West but as an alternative. I don't think that Putin has fully elaborated what that position is. He's tried a lot of different ideas over the years. He's had this idea of "sovereign democracy" in the 1990s, and that evolved into a sponsorship for basically all the populist movements where he can claim leadership of a kind of social conservatism that is allegedly based on Christian values and the family. Whether this is really honest on his part is hard to say because, for example, opposition to abortion, which is important to most Christian groups in Western countries, is really not an issue in Putin's Russia. That being said, he's now found a place as leading an international alliance of populist organizations, including many in the United States. That's a very different configuration of world politics.

This is truly gloomy, but you have recently said that the big question is whether there can be long-term historical progress. You said that you remain optimistic about this.[7] Do you think you will be able to defend this position?

Yes, there are a lot of reasons why democracy is a better system and functions better. It really does provide prosperity, and it also provides accountability, and people want those things. And so even if other systems can override some of the constraints democracy imposes, in the long run these constraints are there for a reason. There's lots of options, but you may not be sure if they're as good as liberal democracy.

Liberal democracy is thriving in some parts of the world even if we get another impression here in Europe. We may probably divide this into two different types of democracies, emerging democracies and old established democracies, like the European version of democracy. Larry Diamond, a Stanford colleague of yours, says in his book *Ill Winds* that he has concerns, but he is also optimistic.[8] Do you share his views? Are there good reasons to be optimistic if you're looking at the world picture of democracies?

The world picture is very mixed. There are very hopeful signs in a certain sense. Prior to the COVID-19 crisis, the world had never looked better because you've had economic growth, hundreds of millions of people lifted out of poverty in developing countries, and by and large you have stability in many parts of the world. In terms of democracies, you've seen a clear rejection of authoritarian government in many countries. You see this in the protests against Nicolás Maduro in Venezuela, against Daniel Ortega in Nicaragua, in Armenia, in Sudan, in Ethiopia, in Belarus, and in Algeria. All of these countries have lived under pretty brutal dictatorships, and there's a clear rejection by civil society in those countries.

The problem we've had over the years is that, when you move from protest against an authoritarian government that's widely disliked to actually establishing democratic institutions, this is a very difficult transition for many countries to make, but I think the impulse that we saw in 1989 in Eastern Europe is still alive in many other parts of the world. We've seen a remarkable revival of protest after the killing of George Floyd in May 2020, not just in the United States but in many other parts of the world. These protests are driven by young people who have distinct political views.

Rising Populism Uses Democratic Legitimacy to Undermine Liberal Institutions

We will have plenty of time to cover the illnesses of mature democracies, but as you say, there is hope. If we look at your work, you have been associated in your youth with what was called the neoconservatives, and you broke with them after the invasion of Iraq. And you also did not like the economic policies that finally led to the financial crisis. What were your main concerns?

The first was about American power and how it could be used to democratize the world, and the second was this idea that markets were self-regulating and that you didn't need a state to watch over them. I think the disasters that followed both of these events showed that these ideas really needed to be rethought. Also, the increasing liberalization of the global economy resulted in a huge increase in actual inequality in the United States and in Britain, the two countries that led this liberal revolution. It was becoming clear that this level of inequality was not sustainable, that there would be some kind of a social revolution if things weren't getting better across the board for ordinary people as well.

At the same time, the Republican Party was moving to the right in a way that I really didn't like at all. After Barack Obama's election, quite frankly, the fact that we elected a Black man president really drove a lot of conservatives crazy. And they started to get more and more extreme in their opposition to Obama, like in the debate over Obama's health care initiative, which I just thought was completely crazy. The United States is the only rich country that doesn't have a universal health care system, seventy years after the rest of Europe had put this in place. And the Republicans say this is socialism and un-American.

When I read your publications, I don't see you as a deeply conservative person. I see you more in line with what I would say would be a European classical liberal.

I think that I accept what you're saying.

You don't have to tell me what you voted for because that doesn't matter.

I'm happy to tell you who I voted for. I voted twice for Obama, and I voted for Hillary Clinton. I voted for the Democratic candidate, Joe Biden, in 2020.

The 2016 election made it clear that liberal democracies face several challenges. In my view, there is one external and two internal threats currently facing liberal democracies. The external threat is authoritarian success—competing political order. The first of the internal threats is the erosion, or even destruction, of institutions, especially those guaranteeing the rule of law. The second internal threat is the lack of mutual respect—losing faith in liberal democracies. This challenge is more "subtle," as it concerns the destruction of the conditions for recognition and loss of faith in liberal democracies. It can also imply the destruction of possibilities for criticism and possibilities of finding viable political solutions. Do you agree with this classification?

I would put it a little bit differently. I think the third threat is a particular kind of populism that has arisen in a lot of democracies and that basically uses democratic legitimacy to undermine liberal institutions.

* * *

After the publication of *Identity* and the thirtieth anniversary of the fall of the Berlin Wall, Fukuyama has been thinking through social and political changes since he wrote his famous essay. We will explore them in the next chapters.

Notes

1. Fukuyama, *Origins of Political Order*, 325.
2. Fukuyama, *End of History*, 293.
3. Freedom House, *Freedom in the World 2019: Democracy in Retreat*.
4. Huntington, *Third Wave*.
5. Diamond, *Ill Winds*.
6. Holmes and Krastev, *Light That Failed*.
7. "Fiscal Crisis Erodes EU Legitimacy."
8. Diamond, *Ill Winds*.

TWO

How Have World Politics Changed?

An important shift in politics has taken place during the last decades. Identity politics has become more pronounced, and political parties that emphasize identity attract voters to a greater extent than political parties that formed the earlier Left–Right economic policy axis. Globalization has helped many countries but has also created greater economic inequality in the Western world. Fukuyama was asked by the *Journal of Democracy* to reflect on the thirty years since the Berlin Wall crumbled. This resulted in an article titled "30 Years of World Politics: What Has Changed?"[1] In this article Fukuyama outlines six underlying trends that have changed world politics: a reorientation of the political axis from economics to identity, a technology shift from being democratic to becoming Big Brother, a loss of status for mediating institutions and the press, a decline in trust, the consequences of neoliberalism, and the ramifications of US policy mistakes. We have touched on some of these already and will be returning to many of these trends during our conversation, but we start by looking at the broader picture of world politics.

The Axis Has Shifted to Identity Politics

In the twentieth century, we had the Left and the Right in politics. Fukuyama argues that this axis has now shifted to an axis of identity. His book *Identity* was a reaction to populism, and he argues that identity is a main driver of current political developments.

Identity politics is not new, but its current political expression—and the polarization it leads to—is. Can you explain what you mean with this shift in politics from 1989?

The fundamental shift is the global axis of world politics moving from being defined by a Left and a Right by economic ideology. That image of Left and Right was largely the nature of politics in the twentieth century. You have a Left that wanted redistribution through a powerful government that could tax and provide social benefits to the people, and you had a Right that was interested in free markets, individual freedom, and a more limited state. The world that I grew up in was defined by this polarity.

And what has changed?

We are increasingly now in a world that is defined by an axis of identity. The world defined by identity is perhaps best summed up by President Donald Trump, who in the midterm elections in the United States back in 2018 could have campaigned on traditional Republican policies like tax cuts, the fact that the economy was producing jobs, or economic growth, but instead he did not talk about that. What did he talk about? He talked about an army of immigrant invaders that were coming up from Mexico, crossing the southern border, and he talked about sending troops. To meet this supposed threat, he was threatening to take away birthright citizenship, and he essentially said that the country was under attack by foreigners. This is a major shift in the nature of American conservatism away from the free market ideology that defined the conservatism of Ronald Reagan. This is the shift from an economic axis to an identity axis. It's not limited to the United States, although I think we all became aware of this as a political trend in 2016 when Donald Trump was elected and when the British voted to leave the European Union. It is appearing in many different places. In Europe you are very much aware because you have two members of the European Union, Hungary and Poland, that have shifted very heavily in this populist direction. Hungary is probably the clearest case, under Viktor Orbán's Fidesz party. All of this is actually not a problem for democracy but for liberal democracy because the tendency of these populist leaders is to say, "I won the election, so I have legitimacy," and they proceed to undermine rule of law institutions.

Do you see this shift elsewhere in the world?

Further afield you have India under Prime Minister Narendra Modi. India was established in the late 1940s as a liberal state. India is an unbelievably diverse country, by religion, by region, and by language. The only way you can run a country that's so diverse and complex is through a liberal system of laws and rules. India had a liberal national identity that was the inheritance from Mahatma Gandhi and Jawaharlal Nehru. But Mr. Modi has been trying to shift that identity away from that idea of a liberal India to one based on Hindu nationalism, which the founders had explicitly rejected. The consequences are things like the citizenship law that the Bharatiya Janata Party passed last year. This made it much harder to become an Indian citizen if you happen to be Muslim. That means the exclusion of up to 200 million Indian citizens who are Muslim.

This is going on in many different parts of the world. I can see this in the kind of militant Buddhism that has arisen in Sri Lanka and Myanmar. You can see it in Latin America, where traditional populism has been left wing but where we have an example of a right-wing populist, Jair Bolsonaro, who was elected president of Brazil in 2018. Latin America is a region that typically has left-wing populists like Hugo Chávez, but for the first time you have a right-wing populist who actually much more explicitly than Donald Trump talks in racist terms about Black Brazilians.

How has this displayed itself in the United States?

You have to look at the demographics of the way people vote. The left-wing party's biggest single base was the working class. The Democrats counted on white working-class voters to win elections. The New Deal coalition continued up to Ronald Reagan, but then motivations shifted, partly due to the way that the Democratic Party has shifted on racial issues toward civil rights, feminism, and so forth. This change started to turn off some of those white working-class voters, and that process has continued. The Left began to redefine itself and was more preoccupied with injustices being done to specific groups of people rather than the working class itself. For many people on the Left, the working class became part of the problem. Over time, a lot of left-wing parties both in the United States and in Europe began to lose support of working-class white voters. A lot of white nationalists will say, "We white people are now a victimized minority. We have been mistreated by affirmative action programs. We can't get our children to the right kinds of schools because the Left favors foreigners over us." This has led to a pretty poisonous kind of politics.

Further, a lot of working-class people are quite culturally conservative. It has to do with race because, before the 1960s, the Democratic Party was built around a big coalition of very disparate groups. They consisted of trade unions, of intellectuals and progressives in the north, but also southern racists who were a big part of the party during the 1930s when Franklin Roosevelt was president. Then, beginning in the 1960s, the Democratic Party broke on race and embraced civil rights legislation. The party tied itself to civil rights, and this change led to the migration of southern racists to the Republican Party.

This is actually the shift from economic self-interest to politics based on identity?

Yes, I believe there is a tendency to want to identify with people who are like you. You may have heard of this famous Stanford study that took place back in the 1950s. They took these two very homogeneous groups of adolescent boys and divided them into two teams and said, you're on the red team, and you're on the blue team. The red team had these characteristics that were completely made up, and by the end of the study they were all trying to kill each other because there's just this tendency to want to identify with someone like yourself. It doesn't have to be by race or ethnicity; it could be by any distinguishing characteristic. I think a lot of people are trying to wrestle with this. And a lot of the polarization in our politics is emotional in a way that defies economic rationality. People are voting against their own self-interest. Obamacare was very good for a lot of southern rural voters, but many voted for Republican politicians. Even if they didn't have health insurance, they voted against it. It does not make much sense, but that's what it means when identity overpowers economic self-interest.

How do you explain this false consciousness; why does identity "trump" economic self-interest?

A lot of Republicans are not necessarily very loyal to the Republican Party, but they hate the idea of a Democrat, who for them is a certain kind of person—a feminist, a gay person, a politically correct person, all these different epithets that they don't like—so they'll vote for anybody who identifies as Republican. Modern economics is based on the theory of everyone's rational self-interest, but a lot of social psychology literature tells you this theory isn't true. People start out with certain ideological or cultural commitments and then they use all of their brain power to justify those positions.

Inequality, Erosion of Trust, and Resentment Lead to Political Shift

Globalization has often been blamed for creating inequality. I would like to hear how you explain the rise in inequality.

Let me just start with the classic approach for all who took a trade theory course. You would have learned that free trade makes everyone richer in the aggregate, but what the professor should have told you, which some people didn't listen to all that carefully, was that not every individual in every country is better off as a result. Indeed, workers in rich countries are losing jobs and opportunities to similarly skilled workers in developing countries. As China and India developed rising middle classes and pulled people out of poverty, you have stagnation in South Carolina.

This resentment among workers in rich countries is obviously part of the explanation for the recent shift in politics, but you have also talked about another slow-moving trend, the decrease of trust.

Yes, this populism goes together with a broad erosion of trust in institutions. I wrote a book back in the 1990s called *Trust*. Trust is intangible and yet critical for the functioning of a society. The idea that you treat other citizens honestly permits free circulation of information, it promotes social cooperation, and by all measures trust in modern societies has been declining—trust in labor unions, political parties, churches, corporations, governments, even families.

If you look at survey data over the last fifty years, levels of trust in virtually all of these institutions have declined, and this has been going on across many countries over the same period of time as the rise in inequality. Basically, this is what Robert Putnam wrote about in his *Bowling Alone* book back in the 1990s about the United States. But while the decline of trust is worrisome, it can be seen as the by-product of good things that have been happening around the world.

But is the loss of trust in authorities and more transparency in general only negative?

No, this is a complicated phenomenon because part of the reason for this erosion of trust has to do with certain positive developments. For example, over the last thirty years, the levels of education in many countries have been rising, and with higher levels of education, people are more skeptical about authority. They question things more, they have more information, and as a result they're less trusting of what they're told by authorities. We have, for instance, had many scandals involving sexual predation by Catholic priests. I don't think that this is a new phenomenon by any means, but we are more aware of it because there's more transparency in the dealings of the Church with its congregation.

Our societies are also becoming more diverse. Another example is the old boys' network, where you had very homogeneous groups of people who went to the same schools and moved in the same social circles. They trusted each other, and that's broken down with women and people from very different backgrounds entering some of these elite circles. Heterogeneity tends to weaken the kinds of bonds of trust that existed in these old networks of older white men that used to run the world. As a result, there's less trust, but the increase in diversity is a good thing. It means that the society is opening up and is becoming in many ways more just. This erosion of trust weakens organizations but also is a necessary component of the larger shifts going on in societies.

Neoliberalism Has Shaped the Global Economy

Some attribute this lack of trust to the economic system of the so-called Chicago school. Do you agree with this criticism, and can you explain neoliberalism?

Neoliberalism is a pejorative term that's usually used to critique a certain approach to policies associated with the Chicago school. The set of ideas that we now call neoliberalism is distinct from classical liberalism. It is more extreme. It is built upon a dogmatic dislike of the state, and as a result we've had economic deregulation that ultimately led to the financial crisis and also to the widening of income disparities.

Who belonged to the Chicago school?

The Chicago school was led by economists like Milton Friedman, George Stigler, Gary Becker, and Robert Lucas. A whole series of very illustrious Nobel laureate economists were part of this movement that in the 1970s and '80s began to dominate economics and the social sciences in a school like Stanford. Many of my colleagues at Stanford are rational choice political scientists, using a model that came out of the Chicago school for understanding human behavior.

How does the Chicago school understand human behavior?

It's based on a highly individualistic understanding of humans. Everyone is an atomized individual. We have preferences and can maximize them through rational decisions, and by this view you can construct human behavior out of those building blocks. The social aspects of human interaction are downplayed in this model. This whole group of orthodox economists developed a very elaborate, although ultimately very simple, model of human behavior. Gary Becker at one point said that this rational utility maximizing model was sufficient to explain all aspects of human behavior and that if you didn't believe that, you were just being lazy and should learn to apply the model more rigorously. It led to a series of policy preferences that privileged markets over governments. What emerged was not liberalism but neoliberalism. In fact, the political rise of Ronald Reagan and Margaret Thatcher was greatly facilitated by the intellectual support given to them by this particular school of economics.

We also had a liberalization in Norway, which was needed in the 1980s.

Liberalization had many good effects because the 1970s governments were overly intrusive. There was too much regulation and unsustainable fiscal policies. But liberalization also had some very negative effects that we are now seeing playing out because of this pure market competition unregulated by governments. It was carried too far. The rise of global inequality is a result of globalization and was the by-product of economic theories that said that free trade and free markets will in the aggregate make everybody richer. That was true, but many didn't pay attention to the part of neoliberalism that said that most unskilled people in rich countries are going to suffer because they will have to compete against similarly educated people in poor countries, and that's exactly what happened with the entry of China into the World Trade Organization. Back then economists said we'll just com-pensate the losers, but that compensation never happened. And that's really what starts the ball rolling with deindustrialization and the de-cline of the working class. Neoliberalism led to a kind of ideological antistatism, and it's not an accident that neoliberalism occurred in the United States, because the United States has a political culture that's always been suspicious of the state, and that kind of American politi-cal tradition dominated discourse in the social sciences.

You paint a quite negative picture of this kind of thinking, and you are implying that it had huge political consequences, at least in the Anglo-Saxon world.

Yes, Reagan and Thatcher were elected in the late 1970s and early '80s, and they were the political expression of neoliberalism. But that movement would not have had such power if it didn't have this high-brow kind of intellectual horsepower behind it, with the economists making quite sophisticated series of policies that really began to shape the global economy in a very serious way. For example, I didn't know this until recently, when I started doing antitrust research for a little project on democracy and the internet at my institute. There was pretty vigorous antitrust enforcement in the United States up until the 1980s. Then professors at the University of Chicago, like Robert Bork and George Stigler, began writing about how those antitrust laws were being misapplied, and they were being used to punish large com-panies that were just being efficient. This led to a gigantic shift in American law.

Now you have two entire generations of judges in the United States who have grown up with these Chicago school assumptions that size really is not something that anyone needs to worry about. As a result, the American corporate sector has grown more and more concentrated over the years. In fact, European consumer prices used to be higher than American ones almost across the board in the 1990s, and now it is the opposite. I think most Europeans who would visit the United States notice that everything's more expensive in the United States— telephones, pharmaceuticals, airline tickets. There's an economist at New York University, Thomas Philippon, who has written an interesting book, *The Great Reversal: How America Gave Up on Free Markets*, in which he says this is the case because Europeans actually took competition policy seriously and forced a lot of markets open, whereas Americans went in the opposite direction and made it possible to concentrate economic power.[2] The reason that antitrust laws don't get enforced is that these companies hire lobbyists who make sure members of Congress don't vote for vigorous antitrust enforcement.

* * *

The Chicago school, and the neoliberal ideas that came from it, gave intellectual credentials to politicians and led to the financial crises in 2008. These structural changes made millions of people lose their jobs and homes, which obviously triggered a great deal of resentment. But we have not seen a strong left-wing populist movement rise up; instead, we have right-wing populism.

Notes

1. Fukuyama, "30 Years of World Politics."
2. Philippon, *Great Reversal.*

THREE

How Do Illiberal Attacks Threaten Democracy?

I lliberal attacks are undermining institutions in established democracies. Turning to Europe, it is easy to see political leaders who are siding with Trump: Viktor Orbán of Hungary, Nigel Farage of Britain, Marine Le Pen of France, and other right-wing populists as well as Recep Erdoğan in Turkey and Vladimir Putin in Russia. Poles and Hungarians are emphasizing their national identity and excluding people who don't share the same historical and cultural background or ethnicity. National identity is being tapped by populist leaders who play on fears. As the Czech writer Milan Kundera has written about small countries, "A small nation is one whose very existence may be put in question at any moment; a small nation can disappear, and it knows it."[1] Before talking about these European countries, Fukuyama explains populism.

Populism and Polarization Block the Political System

In our conversation, Fukuyama mentions two articles he wrote in *The American Interest* from November 2017, "What Is Populism?" and "Why Populist Nationalism Now." In these, he considers three forms of populism. The first is economic populism, which means that a leader (often left wing) proposes economic reforms that are unsustainable over time. Hugo Chávez of Venezuela was a classic example. The second form of populism is about style and charismatic leadership and a close connection with the people: "I represent you." However, this is not an institutional understanding of representation, and often it is in direct opposition to institutions such as the judiciary or the media. The last form of populism involves a particular understanding of the people that excludes people who are different even though they are citizens.

This last form of populism is what we are seeing in Hungary?

Yes, an example is Viktor Orbán's populism in Hungary. He has argued for what he calls illiberal democracy—that is, a majoritarian democracy unconstrained by the constitutional checks and balances, which we associate with the liberal order. Further, he has been trying to redefine Hungarian national identity in ethnic terms—being Hungarian means being ethnically Hungarian, whether you live in Hungary or not, which is fine as long as you're Hungarian. There are two problems with this. There are a lot of non-ethnic Hungarians in the country, and there's several million Hungarians living in neighboring countries in Central and Eastern Europe who are also part of that identity but citizens of other countries. This was also the situation of Germany in the 1930s, which led to World War II. The left-wing populism is usually concentrated on economics and leadership style, and the right-wing populism is more about charismatic leadership and the ethnic understanding of who the people are.

This development creates polarization between "us" and "them," and it influences how politics works. Are we channeling our energies in the direction of identity politics, which somehow drives us to be concerned about who we are, instead of what we can do or agree upon?

I think that polarization is a real problem in many democracies. People are so angry at each other and unwilling to discuss and compromise. That blocks the political system from being able to do anything, and it will get worse. When you are blocking things, you can just continue blaming one another, and you won't be going anywhere.

What is the basis for populist movements?

I think populist movements aren't based on poor people. They're based on people who thought that they were in the middle class, and they've been losing status. It's a relative thing.

Losing status?

It's not poor people who are driving this development. Usually the people at the bottom of the income ladder vote for the left-wing parties, and the people that are in the middle that are losing status have been voting for the right-wing parties.

Orbán is calling Hungary an illiberal democracy—when I first heard about it, I thought about all the countries that had democracy in their name and were absolutely not democracies—but this phenomenon is new. What do you think can explain this development?

Actually, it's not new. Fareed Zakaria wrote an article back in the 1990s saying that the supposedly democratic revolution really wasn't a liberal democratic revolution. It was a revolution where countries were becoming illiberal democracies. That idea has been around for a long time.

Are you saying that these countries don't want to accept liberalism and only have democracy, that is, not liberal democracy?

I think that is basically right. These countries accept the fact that legitimacy comes from the people, but in these countries the people don't want a liberal order that restrains power and forces respect for minority rights and enforces the law in an impartial fashion.

Populist Leaders Undermine the Rule of Law and Constitutions

Let us concentrate on Europe and the rise of populism. What are we witnessing in Poland and Hungary?

The real danger of populism is that a lot of populist leaders want to use their legitimacy to undermine critical institutions, like the rule of law or independent media and the impersonal bureaucracy. They say, "Do we actually need all these laws or constitutional constraints when that's getting in the way of our agenda?" If you are a charismatic leader and think you have a mandate from the people to carry out their will, and you are criticized by newspapers or television channels, or the courts are telling you that you can't do something, or even if you can't get the bureaucracy to prosecute your political enemies, then you try to undermine those institutions. This last thing is deeply worrying, when, for instance, in Poland the Law and Justice party goes about trying to undermine the independence of the judiciary, because that's a permanent change that will really affect the quality of democracy in Poland in the long run. All these right-wing parties are happy to undermine independent judiciaries and delegitimate independent media when it suits them. That's the kind of damage we need to resist.

These internal threats to democracy are preoccupying intellectuals in Western democracies. David Runciman's *How Democracy Ends* is one of many examples. He argues that the way it will go is not sudden death but slow erosion. Do you agree?

A number of political scientists have pointed out how democracy in this latest period of recession has retreated in a different way than in the 1960s and '70s. Back then a series of military coups suddenly replaced democratic rule. Now, it is a slow erosion, especially of the liberal norms of a liberal democracy, that occurs gradually to the point that the ruling party can then change the basic rules to make it extremely difficult for it to ever be removed from power. This is why to me the most worrying thing in some of the oldest democracies is the turn away from liberal international governments and liberal domestic government.

Why do you think we tend to call these quite destructive parties and leaders populists?

It is partly a definitional thing. We tend to call people that undermine institutions populists. And so almost by definition they're going to do these destructive things. If we like what they're doing, and they don't attack institutions, we just call them democratically elected leaders. It is kind of a circular reasoning. I would say that rather than necessarily using a label like populist, you need to consider whether particular leaders are actually willing to operate within a constitutional framework and respect the rule of law.

Why is it that the democratic system has left this room for populists to tap into?

This is an interesting long-term question about democracy because a lot of political scientists believe that at a certain point democracy consolidates, and then it's really not possible to go backward. I think that we've seen a number of democracies, including the United States, going backward in many ways. And the reasons probably vary from one society to another, but partly it is the emergence of very opportunistic leaders who see an opening for themselves to gain power because of failures in the current political leadership. For example, if you didn't have the financial crisis in the United States, and if Europe had not suffered the euro crisis and the migrant crisis, you might not have had populism. But the political elites oftentimes screw up and misunderstand what to do, and as a result people are just justifiably angry with them.

The 1960s and '70s also had populists. What is different now?

I think that back in the 1960s and '70s you had a very energized Left that was still Marxist, and you had a radical fringe in every European country. This time you have a radical Right actually questioning a lot of the more fundamental premises.

But are these populists only doing bad things?

No, sometimes the populists are pushing for things that are popular and perhaps even necessary. The Law and Justice party in Poland has enacted a family subsidy. That's extremely popular among Poles. The previous government said no, we can't afford it, but it's something that has proven to be quite successful, and it helps to legitimate the party.

So, if you have the money and can finance your reforms, the populists will stay popular?

Yes, but think about Viktor Orbán. He gets subsidies from the European Union. Five percent of the Hungarian gross domestic product is from the European Union, and that is crazy. If you took that away from him, he would not look like a successful leader of a democratic country.

These populists are also saying that they are democratically elected, that they represent the people, but I believe that the single most valuable trait of

Norwegian democracy is the ability to form compromises. These populists are not into compromise.

You are right, they don't compromise. Democracy is an institution that seeks to reconcile differences in a pluralistic society. But it doesn't mean that it necessarily is going to work all the time. Social conflicts get to a certain point where you have fundamental disagreements on basic values. No set of rules is going to contain that, and compromise is hard. The question is whether we are approaching that period in Europe, and I don't think we're quite there yet, because there is still a fairly strong consensus about the rule of law, democracy, and basic values. But it's definitely being challenged in ways that are different from earlier challenges. I guess the thing that I take a little bit of comfort from is that most of the populists when they get into power, they really screw things up, as in the current COVID-19 crisis.

If you compare what we are experiencing in a historical perspective, how bad is the political situation today?

I think we need to put this in a little bit of perspective. It's not as if these kinds of setbacks are new. Throughout the twentieth century, we were constantly having big setbacks to democracy, much bigger than we've experienced in the last decade. The 1930s was not a great decade for democracy, and we still managed to recover. We still have agency. This is not an inevitable trend, and authoritarian government is not inexorably on the rise. People can put a stop to it by going out in the streets and protesting and ultimately by voting. Protesting is harder in an age of COVID-19, but it will come back. The massive protests that broke out in Belarus in late August 2020 after the country's dictator, Aleksandr Lukashenko, stole an election after performing miserably in the face of the COVID-19 shows that the spirit of 1989 continues to live in authoritarian countries.

Citizens Forget What It Means
to Live under Authoritarian Rulers

The rule of law is paramount, and liberal democracies, which are built on the rule of law and have noncorrupt and independent institutions, are in a better position to counter strong pressure from various interest groups and to fend off authoritarian tendencies.

How can the rule of law be protected in countries where leaders with authoritarian inclinations are elected democratically?

The only way you can protect the rule of law is by winning elections. That's the way power is distributed in a democracy. If you keep losing elections to these people, they will continue to entrench themselves. That's really the only route. Probably it's a hard thing, especially if the information that the voters get is not sufficient, but the world as a whole is really not that bleak a place. If you look at the things that have been happening all over the world lately, you have Nicaragua, Armenia, Ukraine, Sudan, and Algeria. Ethiopian prime minister Abiy Ahmed got the Nobel Peace Prize, and you have Hong Kong. All these countries demonstrate that populations really do not like authoritarian governments. They may not be able to agree on what replaces an authoritarian government, but they don't like living under a dictatorship.

What about developments in democracies that seem to go in authoritarian directions? In 1989, I met a lot of young students from Eastern European countries. They were so keen on going to Western Europe, but they are older now and their kids were born after 1989. Do you think that it has a lot to do with it?

Yes, the memory of what it means to live in a real authoritarian country has disappeared. It's a curious thing.

You described this phenomenon to a Danish interviewer in 2019:

> Look at Poland. It was one of the former Eastern Bloc countries that most successfully escaped the grip of Soviet communism and rapidly became a part of Europe and a stable democracy. Poland before the rise of the Law and Justice party was the most successful European member of the European Union, with high economic growth, and yet the voters elect this party. But today the majority was born after the fall of the wall, and they have no experience with living in an authoritarian regime.

They can take life in a modern democratic society for granted. And suddenly the discontent rises because democracy is not enough. Then the criticism of the EU begins, and fear of immigration, things that were not an issue when Poland was under a communist dictatorship.[2]

Do you believe humans have a fundamental resentment of tyranny and people do not want political authorities who violate their fundamental rights?

It depends. If you're the subject of authoritarian repression, you don't like it. Nobody likes that. But, on the other hand, it depends on the agenda of the authoritarian. If you're part of the majority community that's trying to enforce your will on a minority, then you will not necessarily think it is bad.

But you have also said that nobody wants to go to China to live there.

That's true. That's why I think people have to experience authoritarian repression personally or see it around them before they realize that it's a bad thing. I think that it's been a generation since you've had real authoritarian government in Europe.

Coming back to Ivan Krastev, the coauthor of *The Light That Failed*, he also wrote *After Europe* in 2017 where he talks about Eastern Europe, especially the rise of nationalism and also demographic challenges. He says that people moved to Western countries to get a better life and that many thought their societies quickly would become liberal and capitalist, but in Germany it was different. In 2010 Berlin hosted the first exhibition dedicated to Hitler, and in the middle of Berlin, you find the Jewish memorial Denkmal. The Germans have another approach?

Postwar Germany invested a lot in teaching the next generation the truth of what had happened during the Holocaust, not seeking either to portray themselves as Hitler's victims as Austria did or to ignore that history altogether as Japan has largely done with its colonial legacy in Asia. This effort to inculcate liberal values was so broad and persistent that many younger Germans began to resent this lecturing, but it had an effect. None of the states in Eastern Europe confronted their wartime histories as honestly, with the result that younger generations are not necessarily imbued with the kinds of liberal values that Germans possess.

Are there other reasons for the illiberal tendencies that we see in Europe, that many want to "get a voice," "be heard and understood," "want security more than freedom"?

If they choose, well, it may be part of it. It may be just a random mobilization of people by particular leaders. If you didn't have Trump or Orbán, both those countries would have been very different. But it's surprising in a way that this hasn't happened earlier given the sorts of things we've had, the financial crisis and so forth. Why did it all of a sudden take off in 2016? I don't think you can just explain this in terms of structural forces. Leadership matters rather a lot.

* * *

The gradual disappearance of memories of authoritarian society is disturbing to me as a historian, and it is of course also disappointing when I think about the optimism created after 1989. Fukuyama describes the mechanisms that drive populism; among them, the destruction of the rule of law and the constitution are among the most serious issues. We now turn to Fukuyama's own country, the United States.

Note

1. Quoted in Holmes and Krastev, *Light That Failed*, 39.
2. "Fukuyama: Populismen peger paa ægte problemer, man har forkerte svar."

FOUR

Will the US Cease to Be the Beacon of the Liberal Order?

We cannot end our discussion of populism and its consequences without discussing the United States and the election of Donald Trump in 2016 and what has followed. This election has had a seismic effect on American society, American international relations, and on the special position of the United States in the global system since World War II. *Identity* was the direct consequence of the election of Donald Trump as president of the United States in 2016.

The Election of Trump Speaks to a Deeper Polarization in American Society

How did you react when Trump won?

I was horrified; I did not expect it. But I also thought that it would be an interesting test of American institutions because in many ways the Constitutional system was designed to constrain somebody like Donald Trump.

How would you describe Trump and his presidency?

In 2020 we have been preoccupied with the COVID-19 crisis, and it has been a singular misfortune for the United States to have been led by Donald Trump in this period of national emergency. His lack of qualification to be a national leader has been on public display. For more than two months he denied that there was even a crisis and did nothing to prepare the country for the pandemic. As a result, we currently have the world's highest number of COVID-19 deaths and are in one of the steepest recessions in living memory. Today America's performance is lagging that of Europe by a huge amount, and Trump is pretending that the crisis is over.

What is most disturbing about the Trump phenomenon is that so many Americans were willing to vote for him. And 35 to 40 percent of the American people didn't just vote for him, they really love him fanatically. He's created this cult of personality, which I find extremely troubling. The cult-like adulation of this man is something I really never expected I would witness in the United States, and it makes you wonder about the judgment of your fellow citizens, but there it is. He's really not a good person. Describe him, for example, for children for future generations, and it's very hard to imagine somebody that's a worse example than Trump in every single dimension. You want to teach your children to be honest, you want them to have this larger sense of moral purpose, you want them to have a core to their personality other than themselves, and this guy manages to violate every single character trait that is desirable in human beings. I guess this is the thing that I've had the hardest time dealing with. I've had great faith in democracy, but particularly in American democracy, that people can vote for stupid things in the short run, but eventually they would come around to correcting their mistakes and making wiser choices.

Although Joe Biden won in November, problems are not solved?

The outcome of the election speaks to a deeper polarization in American society. The Democrats did not win an overwhelming victory against Trump and Trumpism. Probably the biggest weakness of our system right now is the fact that many Republicans think that the Democratic Party is a bigger threat to their way of life than Russia, which I find completely incomprehensible. Trump has convinced a big majority of the Republican Party to accept him. That's probably the most disappointing thing. He was even acquitted by the Republican Party in the impeachment hearings, despite the fact that he was clearly guilty as charged. You have a lot of Republicans that should realize the kind of threat he poses to our institutions, but because of a kind of cynical calculation that he will get them things that they want, they're willing to accept him.

What do you think about the changes in the Republican Party over time?
Did you once vote Republican?

During the 1980s I voted for Reagan and George H. W. Bush and served in two Republican administrations, but I didn't vote for George W. Bush in 2004. I switched parties when I moved to California in 2010 and registered as a Democrat. I did this because the Republican Party had changed beyond recognition with the rise of the Tea Party. The Republican Party I admired was the party of the elder Bush, and people like James Baker, Brent Scowcroft, and the like, all of whom were strong internationalists and believers in democracy. In a period when I was moving to appreciate much better the importance of having a capable modern state, the Tea Party was shifting the Republicans in the opposite direction, to undermining and delegitimizing the state.

At Stanford we have the Hoover Institution, which is a classical Republican conservative think tank, and they were mostly George Bush Republicans, on the right but not far right of center. They believe in free markets, and they were all in favor of relatively liberal immigration policy and so forth, and when Trump was elected, many of them were horrified. But quite a number have now become big supporters. I think the reason is a kind of moral compromise in which they say we wanted deregulation, and we wanted better federal judges, and he's delivered that, so we like his economic policies, and they don't think about the cultural things.

Is this disappointing to you?

Yes, many of my Republican friends have been disappointing. It really annoys me because a lot of them have made compromises with their principles. I have talked to them in private and they say, "Well, we don't like Trump," but then publicly they don't say anything critical of him.

How has your life changed after the election of Donald Trump?

You know, I find Donald Trump so obnoxious that I have become more political by following day-to-day politics. It's been a preoccupation not just of mine but of a lot of people. In earlier phases of my life, politics was a little bit more normal. I would say that more has happened in the past few years that was unanticipated, at least by me and most of the people I know, than in the previous twenty years.

"The risk of sliding into a world of competitive and equally angry national-isms is huge," you wrote on November 9, 2016, "and if this happens it would mark as momentous a juncture as the fall of the Berlin Wall in 1989."[1]
How does Trump's election relate to the end-of-history thesis? Does it invalidate it?

Well, it's still shocking, and what I didn't really expect was that Trump would actually get worse over time. I expected him to be a bad pres-ident, but I had no idea how bad it would be. In my Political Order books, I had already modified the views in *The End of History* to en-compass the phenomenon of political decay—that is, the possibility that political systems could go backward in terms of development. Trump is a case of that.

I think, largely, institutions have worked: the courts, the media, and the electoral system, and so forth have resisted his attempts to undermine them. But it was not for want of trying. He's attacked his own FBI, his own Justice Department, his own attorneys general, the intelligence community, the bureaucracy. He's called the mainstream media enemies of the American people. Following his acquittal in his impeachment trial, Trump began a purge of his perceived enemies throughout the bureaucracy and a replacement of inspectors general that were meant to keep tabs on abuses. But the most important thing is that Trump is the most incompetent president ever elected.

In *The End of History* you wrote a comment about Trump and his real estate business: "The decline of community life suggests that in the future, we will risk becoming secure and self-absorbed last men . . . but the opposite danger exists as well, namely, that we return to being first men engaged in bloody and pointless prestige battles . . . for are there not reservoirs of idealism that cannot be exhausted—indeed, that are not even touched—if one becomes a developer like Donald Trump."[2] This was back in 1992. You didn't know that Trump twenty-five years later would be president in the United States. In the case of Trump, what happened, according to you? How was the path laid open to his ascent to power?

Well, the path was always open. Anyone can go into politics. I thought Trump wouldn't have a particular interest in doing that. But evidently, he did. It was kind of the only place where he hadn't reached the top. He wanted to climb that as well. He actually failed as a real estate developer. So, in the 2000s he became a reality TV star. But politics was another area where he hadn't really tried his hand yet.

If you're looking back, how would you explain the election of Donald Trump?

In addition to the issue of identity, which we've discussed, we also in the United States have a racial issue, which Trump has been happy to exploit. There are a lot of working-class white people who feel that the America they grew up in is somehow disappearing before their eyes. They don't like it, and he's capitalized on that resentment. And it also has to do with our political system. Well before Donald Trump was elected, the system did not deliver well because of interest groups and lobbyists. There were endless parliamentary discussions and maneuvers among political parties, and they did not make the hard decisions that were necessary to improve the welfare of ordinary people. Over the last couple of decades, there has been political deadlock and increasing polarization. This has led to demands for a strong man and a decisive government that could cut through and get things done.

Is it a kind of accident of history that Trump's desire for that kind of recognition coincided with a sense of loss of recognition on the part of large sections of the electorate, or is that just an unlucky coincidence?

It is just an accident. It didn't have to happen. The vote was really close as well, and the candidate on the other side wasn't up to the task.

Could it have been prevented?

Well, I mean Hillary Clinton could have run a better campaign, and the Democrats could have picked a different candidate. Biden should have run in 2016.

Trump voters are a mix of Christian conservatives, nationalists, and protectionists. How has the division of American voters become different with the election of Donald Trump?

Donald Trump has mobilized a very angry constituency. It's never going to be more than about a third of the country. But they're now quite angry and upset, and even after his presidency, they're not going away as a voting bloc. It's troubling for the future of the country because that's one of the drivers of polarization. He has made this polarization much more visible.

There Will Be Deep Divisions Even after the Democratic Win in the 2020 Election

Your first tweet after it became clear that Joe Biden was the winner of the 2020 election was, "It feels like we've just completed an exorcism." How is it going?

I and many people like me are delighted that Biden won and have been celebrating. But more than 74 million Americans voted for Trump, and there was no Biden landslide as many had been hoping. At this moment Republicans are lining up to support Trump's assertion that the election was stolen, even though there is not a shred of evidence that this is true. So we still have a problem.

What do you think of the long-term situation of the Republican Party in the United States?

It's not good in the very long term because the people who vote for Donald Trump are a declining group within the country as a whole. They're less educated, more rural, have fewer opportunities, and they are declining as a percentage of the population. Down the road, many Republicans understand that they're really on the losing side of a big demographic shift. They are trying desperately to protect their ability to stay in power by disenfranchising voters who would vote Democratic, endorsing gerrymandering, and doing things like disqualifying potential Democratic voters through voter identification laws. But the trouble with these long-term projections is that you have to survive the short term in order to get to them, and that's going to be very difficult.

The two parties are ideologically much more homogeneous now, and in certain ways the Republican Party is becoming a party of older white people, and the Democratic Party is just a very heterogeneous coalition of different minority groups, including progressive women, educated professionals, younger voters, and the like. That's overall not a healthy way for politics to divide because it reinforces the intensity of the fears on both sides. You've got this fear that has resurrected these ghosts of race divisions, and the United States just has such a deep history of racial conflict that it tends to define our politics. To some extent, Trump has normalized a certain racist understanding of race relations in the United States. Look at his reaction to the George Floyd protests—calls to shoot demonstrators—and his defense of Confederate statues.

What are your thoughts for the future of the United States?

Even under Biden's presidency, the United States will still be plagued by political polarization. There will be a good third of the country that will feel angry and resentful, and many have contested the legitimacy of the election, even violently. Biden will be handed a country suffering from disease and a severe economic recession, and the society as a whole will be subject to huge distributional conflicts as the government hands out assistance very broadly.

American Withdrawal from the International Scene Leads to Global Problems

One of the issues you have raised is the US withdrawal from international agreements under Donald Trump. But you are pointing out that it might be the result of a long-term process.

Yes, it is a change in the behavior of the United States. If you think about what was called the international liberal order that we've been living under since the end of World War II, the United States was critical in establishing institutions like the North Atlantic Treaty Organization and the World Trade Organization. It takes one player that is bigger and stronger than all the others in order to actually create these kinds of institutions. That's really the role that the United States has played over the past several decades, but the United States started checking out of this system. It actually started to happen earlier than Trump. Donald Trump is not that different from Barack Obama in terms of foreign policy. Obama really wanted to get out of the Middle East. He wasn't able to, but he wanted to, and he wanted to have US foreign policy focus on Asia. There is more of a continuity between Obama's foreign policy and Trump's foreign policy than either of them would like to admit because, as a result of the failed interventions in Afghanistan and Iraq, a lot of Americans began to wonder why they were being asked to send their sons and daughters to fight and die in these very remote places without an obvious benefit to the United States. The major difference, however, is that Trump has an aversion to multilateral institutions that Obama never did. I expect Biden's policy to be very similar to Obama's, though perhaps more engaged with our European allies.

The interventions in Iraq and Afghanistan are one factor, but there are also economic failures.

Yes, the United States in this thirty-year period made some very big mistakes in both foreign policy and economic policy. The biggest foreign policy mistake was the invasion of Iraq in 2003, which led to long-term American involvement in that region. It was preceded by the invasion of Afghanistan, but the Iraq invasion was more consequential for destabilizing much of the Middle East and leading to the rise of Iran and Shiite power as well as ISIS and other forms of radical Islam. These were all unintended consequences of the Bush administration's invasion of that country. The second-biggest American mistake had its origins in the decisions to deregulate the financial markets, which stretch all the way back to the 1990s. These policy decisions ultimately led to the 2008 financial crisis and led to a big disaster in terms of ordinary people's incomes.

Unfortunately, you had a hegemonic leader in the United States, which, for a twenty-year period between 1989 and 2008, didn't live up to a lot of its responsibilities, and it's important for Americans to understand that. These are some of the rather slow-moving changes that have affected the nature of our world. If you just imagine a counterfactual, that there had been no Iraq intervention, and you had better prudential regulation of the banking sector in the United States, I don't think you would have had the 2008 crisis or have elected Donald Trump. Elites are actually making big mistakes; in the American case, that was definitely true.

If the United States drops out of leading the international system, who's going to take its place, China?

I don't think that's going to be an adequate substitute.

What do you think will be the outcome of the Chinese–American trade war?

China in the long run is going to be a bigger challenge than either Russia or Islamic radicalism because the Chinese know what they're doing. They can create a very powerful modern high-tech economy. They're huge. Dealing with them is going to be really difficult, and the one part of Trump's agenda that a lot of Democrats have supported is being less accommodating with China and using trade as a weapon. It's interesting because I go to Asia a lot. I talked to a lot of pro-democracy people in Asia; a lot of them are Chinese. They love the trade war. They say there's nothing else that's going to get the attention of the Communist Party leadership in China.

Will the United States regain its international hegemonic role under Biden?

I don't think it will be possible for American allies to regain the trust they once had in the American commitment, even under Biden's presidency. They all know that there is still a big populist-isolationist bloc of voters out there and that the old bipartisan consensus on internationalism has broken down. The Republicans could come roaring back in 2022 or 2024. So it will be hard for the United States to resume its old role.

If you put American isolationism into the picture of rising nationalism, will it be even more difficult to succeed in gaining international cooperation?

The rise of nationalism is very bad for international cooperation because, essentially, you're going to look after your own country first. It is a narrowing of time horizons. This tendency is being greatly enhanced by the COVID-19 pandemic and the natural suspicion it raises of foreigners. No nation cooperates with other nations simply out of the goodness of its heart or because it's meeting some kind of moral requirement. You do it out of self-interest. You realize if you don't cooperate with other countries, you're not going to solve global health, or control money laundering, or any of the kinds of problems that the international community faces. It is a question of whether you sacrifice short-term sovereignty for long-term benefits. What we've seen is, especially on the part of the United States, a narrowing of that sense of self-interest in the case of Donald Trump. It's so transactional that, basically, if the United States doesn't make money on a particular agreement, we're simply not going to have any part of it. That's obviously something that is very bad because of the historic role the United States has played.

We can conclude that we are worse off today than thirty years ago?

Yes, I think that increasing protectionism will affect global politics. We are in the process of overcorrecting rising globalism because Donald Trump hasn't wanted to be involved anywhere and hasn't believed in international institutions. That's not very good for global institutions and how they operate. We are racing away from internationalism to the opposite pole, pretty blindly.

* * *

So far it seems that the answer to the question Fukuyama asked in 2017—whether American democracy is strong enough for Trump—is yes, but it is obvious that the political climate in the United States has become more polarized than ever. The underlying problems of American society before the election of Donald Trump emerged under his presidency. The next big trend we will discuss has a lot to do with Trump's rise to power. No president has ever used social media as he has.

Notes

1. "Democracy and Its Discontents."
2. Fukuyama, *End of History*, 328.

FIVE

Will Orwell's *1984* Dystopia Come True?

We have come to the last big change in the three decades since the fall of the Berlin Wall. Some might say it underlies many of the changes that we have seen in democracies, in politics, in labor markets, and in trade—but also in public debate. The roles of traditional and social media have changed dramatically. In *Our Posthuman Future*, Fukuyama says, "It is easy to see what's wrong with the world of *1984*: the protagonist, Winston Smith, is known to hate rats above all things, so Big Brother devises a cage in which rats can bite at Smith's face in order to get him to betray his lover. This is the world of classical tyranny, technologically empowered but not so different from what we have tragically seen and known in human history."[1] And in the same book, he writes, "Information technology, for example, produces many social benefits and relatively few harms, and therefore has appropriately gotten by with a fairly minimal degree of government regulation."[2] This has changed substantially.

The Power of Information, Appropriated by Enemies of Democracy

Clearly, many things have happened since 2002 when you wrote *Our Posthuman Future*. What do you think of social media and the internet today?

There's been a dialectical process. It was really good for democracy in the early days, and a lot of authoritarian leaders got very scared by this. So both Russia and China devised methods of controlling it. The Chinese have figured out how to basically control their internet users so that they do not threaten the regime, and the Russians have figured out how to turn the internet into a weapon they can use against their geopolitical rivals. In both cases the pendulum swung in the other direction, and now there are a lot of domestic actors who have also begun to use social media as a weapon. Now everybody's trying to figure out how to defend themselves against this, and I suspect the pendulum starts to swing back at a certain point.

How do you see the development of information technology?

When the internet first came into popular use in the 1990s, everybody thought this would be great for democracy because information is power. Everyone, myself included, thought this was great for democracy. If you put a computer on everybody's desktop, they're going to be empowered, to have information, and to participate. People would get power, and it would be possible to mobilize, to hold governments accountable, and in fact, a lot of that happened. Most democratic countries now put a tremendous amount of information online, and citizens can see what government is doing, how they're procuring items, how they're dealing with each other. A lot of protest movements could not have existed without supportive social media, but it turns out that the bad guys also figured out how to use these technologies.

Facebook came into being in 2004 with a mission to connect people, but now we are talking about all its negative aspects: power, taxes, algorithms, and so forth. What happened?

We learned in the last few years that the enemies of democracy also figured out how to use technology. You got rid of these hierarchies, the editors, publishers, and mainstream media outlets that used to control what people saw. Anyone can publish anything. The consequence is that you often get bad information, and some of that information is deliberately planted by people who want to undermine their supposed enemies. This is something that Putin's Russia has been able to do in other democratic countries in Europe and America over the last few years.

But there is a contrary trend as well. It's true that anyone can say anything, that people have access to the internet almost universally around the globe. But with the rise of artificial intelligence (AI) and machine learning, we are actually moving in the opposite direction from the original personal computer (PC) revolution. The PC revolution was democratic, spreading computing power to everybody. AI is the opposite. It concentrates the ability to use these technologies in large companies and large countries. It's a big problem with artificial intelligence, particularly with these programs that are able to modify themselves without our intervention. It's not like a car, where you can take it apart down to all the nuts and bolts and put it back together again and know exactly how it works. You have these complex algorithms that are written by other algorithms and you have no idea how it's going up with this result. There's no transparency.

You mentioned Russia, but China is also a player here.

Yes, China has a big advantage because it's got such a big population. It can process petabytes of data that a small country like Norway simply doesn't have access to. China has figured out how to use the internet to control the internet. This is not something that rewards small scale. The only organizations and countries that are really able to make use of this kind of data are large ones, either large countries like China or large corporations, like Facebook and Google. Correspondingly, there's been a shift of power toward either authoritarian states or very large corporations. This I think is itself a long-term threat to democracy.

The combination of size, authoritarian government, and technological possibilities is then poisonous?

Yes, the Chinese have a very comprehensive system of censorship and social control over the use of the internet, and in fact China is now a surveillance state that is able to use the capabilities of modern technology to minutely control the behavior of all of its citizens. And obviously the kind of surveillance state that the Chinese are trying to create is also unprecedented. The Chinese are trying to use all this modern technology that allows them to monitor and control people's behavior in a much more minute way than the Soviet Union ever could. The COVID-19 pandemic has increased the incentives to use this kind of technology to monitor people's contacts, and that is something that is likely to stay with us.

Fake News and Political Interference
Widen Polarization, Create Fear

Fake news has always been around, but with the internet and social media, it can reach millions within seconds. What are your thoughts?

Of course, fake news has always existed. But the speed and scale of its dissemination is far greater now than before the rise of the internet. Further, the private internet platforms have had a commercial interest in virality, and fake news is often the most viral. What the Russians have been doing is often different: rather than manufacturing fake news, they simply accelerate the flow of extremist views being produced by Americans by pretending to be evangelical Christians or Black Lives Matter activists and trying to widen existing polarizations.

The Russians use technology outside their borders to interfere, including in the United States. Why do they do it?

Russia uses technology against its perceived enemies to undermine their confidence in their institutions, to create fear in elections, and to exacerbate polarization among citizens of other democracies like the United States and Britain.

It plays up to the ongoing identity politics we have been talking about?

Yes, the internet has become a source of polarization itself because the internet is perfectly suited to this new form of identity politics where people can talk to other people who share their views. They don't have to listen to other people whose views they disagree with, and it tends to reinforce the compartmentalization of society into these different identity groups, and it weakens any kind of common sense and sense of citizenship.

This polarization has opened the United States up to foreign interference. There's no question that Russia meddled in the 2016 election. Russia's goal is to try to exaggerate the polarization and make it harder for people to trust their governments and their fellow citizens. During the 2016 election, I used to follow a Twitter handle called @TEN_GOP. I thought it belonged to the Tennessee Republican Party, but it turned out it was a troll in St. Petersburg. And they were very good at it because I read this Twitter feed for six months, and I thought it was another American that was writing all their posts. But it was some Russian guy working for the Internet Research Agency.

And if people exclude others in the so-called echo chambers, this goes hand in hand with identity politics?

It allows very small identity groups to find one another and kind of amplifies their sense of separateness. For example, I don't know if you follow this thing about incels, these young men who are involuntarily celibate. Apparently some school shooters had been part of this movement, but who knew that this group existed until a couple of years ago? Apparently, they all found one another on the internet, and they communicate, and they build on each other's grievances. It's a very disturbing phenomenon when you don't even have a common basis of factual information on which you can base democratic deliberation.

We don't have this information polarization in Norway. How has it changed American society?

If you live in America today, you may easily be living in completely separate information spheres. You can live in one universe defined by the *New York Times* or CNN or MSNBC that has one set of facts. If you watch Fox News, you've got a completely different set of facts. Today if you're a Republican, you watch Fox News, you don't believe that global warming is happening. You think this is all a liberal conspiracy. More recently, you don't believe that COVID-19 is a serious problem. If you watch CNN or MSNBC and read the *New York Times*, you think that the conspiracy runs in the other direction. I don't want to make these morally equivalent because they're not—they're much worse on the Right—but I think that this information divide is very much embedded in the extreme degree of polarization we see.

And the power of Facebook does not make it easier to get high-quality information?

Mark Zuckerberg should own up to his responsibilities and basically start censoring advertising on Facebook because he's just too powerful—at least in the short run. These internet platforms have grown big pretending that they're just neutral platforms that simply transmit other people's opinions. But they have a tremendous ability to accelerate certain messages over others. Their basic business is to maximize revenue, and they do that by selling promotions that get clicks. In many countries Facebook and Google are the way that people communicate. There are some countries where you cannot talk to people about politics without going to Facebook. And as a result, you also have this monopoly problem. Facebook basically took over the Philippines through Facebook Basics. A lot of people didn't notice this. Facebook entered the Philippines just a few years ago, and now the percentage of Filipinos on Facebook is like 95 percent. President Rodrigo Duterte, the authoritarian president of the Philippines, is using it to attack his enemies and does it extremely effectively. This is a trend that has just begun.

The Abuses of Biotech Surveillance and Unchecked Monopolies

A quote from *Identity* illustrates your point: "The nice thing about dystopian fiction is that it almost never comes true. That we can imagine how current trends will play themselves out in an ever more exaggerated fashion serves as a useful warning: *1984* became a potent symbol of a totalitarian future we wanted to avoid and helped inoculate us from it."[3] In 2002 you contrasted developments in biological and surveillance technologies in *Our Posthuman Future*; do you still think biotech is a more serious threat?

Well right now biotech is a real problem, and the biotech revolution has been slower to materialize, but it is going to happen. Actually, it is affecting something deeper than social media.

Would you today agree to extensive surveillance if it makes you feel secure?

No, people don't really like that. But again, it's one of those things that goes back and forth where people want security after a terrorist attack, but then they don't like the abuses that come with increased policing. This feeling is even stronger in Europe, where privacy is written into basic law as a fundamental right. This is why GDPR (the General Data Protection Regulations) were enacted, something we need in the United States.

You have argued that Gutenberg, Bell, the printing press, and electricity, have all changed our outlook on the world: are each of these technological revolutions about how we are able to use and understand information?

All of these technological revolutions are similar. You have an innovation. It's very disruptive, and then it takes society a long time to figure out how to deal with the disruption. It wasn't just printing, it was television, radio. And like the steam engine, all of these things produce huge social changes. We're constantly trying to figure out how to adapt to the challenges. The major new technologies that were created in the period from 1870 to 1970 were far more disruptive than anything that's happened since then.

Can we recreate the "Habermasian" public sphere, with authoritative, edited media?[4]

It's going to be much harder, I think, because institutions are not as well trusted as before, and there's less authority behind facts. I'm not quite sure what the path is to restore something like a shared public space. This is the thing: a lot of disinformation is fed by underlying social and political conflicts. If you didn't have a populist movement that was very distrustful of the elite to begin with, fake news wouldn't be so much of a problem. It's effective only because people are motivated to use it in that fashion.

Easy access to information can also make us lazy and unwilling to seek additional viewpoints. Do we have to educate people?

We have a big project now here at Stanford to try to look into all of this, but I think we're way too early to be able to say what the answer to this is going to be. A number of studies have shown that if you are a strong partisan, you will use your cognitive abilities to further encourage yourself. We have this idea we're all rational individuals, and we take information from the outside world, and we develop theories to match that empirical information. Unfortunately, that's not the way it works. Human beings start with strong opinions, and they use their cognitive abilities to justify those opinions. That's why sometimes smarter, educated people are actually more convinced of opinions that are ultimately wrong.

It must in some sense have to do with education and critical thinking?

Maybe, but I'm not sure that's going to be enough. I'm not sure we can actually educate the right people. You're not going to educate all the bad actors and make them think the way you think. So I'm not sure that's really possible. It may be part of the solution, but I don't think it's all. There are other things that will be needed.

What are you thinking could be a solution?

As I mentioned earlier, AI rewards very large companies and countries like China that have access to huge amounts of data. In fact, my current research agenda is looking at competition policy among these internet platforms. It used to be that you had monopolists that could, let's say, monopolize the oil sector, but a company like Amazon can monopolize anything it wants to because it has got this huge amount of consumer data. If they want to move from books to baby diapers to groceries, they can do it. It's a very new concentration of economic power that is not even national because Facebook is the dominant player in over a hundred different countries. And, again, it's a kind of private power that we have not seen previously. That has a lot of troubling dimensions to it. I must say the European Union has been much more active on this front in trying to regulate the internet than the United States has because of America's general reluctance to use state power to regulate the private sector, but it's coming. I have to tell you, in Silicon Valley itself, opinions about the role of companies like Facebook or Google have shifted 180 degrees over the last eighteen months. People used to regard them as basically good for everybody. They gave money, they were good for democracy. Today they face major antitrust suits from the Federal Trade Commission, Justice Department, and state attorneys general.

* * *

For someone like Fukuyama, who grew up with books and has spent his life writing, teaching, and talking about the value of democracy, it must be frustrating to witness how technological developments have contributed to polarization and how the internet has become an immensely powerful tool in the hands of authoritarian regimes, populists, and the FAANG-companies (Facebook, Amazon, Apple, Netflix, and

Google). How Fukuyama became one of the world's most prolific political thinkers is what our dialogue next explores.

Notes

1. Fukuyama, *Our Posthuman Future*, 5.
2. Fukuyama, 11.
3. Fukuyama, *Identity*, 182.
4. Habermas, *Structural Transformation of the Public Sphere*.

SIX

Is Fukuyama a Classical European Liberal?

Francis Fukuyama's paternal grandfather came to the United States in 1905 to escape the Russo-Japanese War. He opened a store in Los Angeles, only to lose it while being interned during World War II. Fukuyama's father, Yoshio, was born in 1921 and was not interned with his family but instead won a scholarship to study in Nebraska. He went on to train as a Congregationalist minister and to receive a doctorate in sociology from the University of Chicago, serving as a faculty member at the Chicago Theological Seminary. In Chicago Yoshio met Toshiko Kawata, who had grown up in Kyoto. She was the daughter of Shiro Kawata, who was a prominent Japanese economist and president of the Osaka Municipal University. They married in 1950, and Francis Fukuyama was born in 1952. He grew up mostly in New York City, until the family moved to State College, Pennsylvania, in 1967.

Francis studied political philosophy and classics under Allan Bloom at Cornell University. He first met Bloom and Paul Wolfowitz when he was living at Telluride House at Cornell. After graduating, Fukuyama went to Paris to study with Jacques Derrida and Roland Barthes. He continued his studies in comparative literature at Yale, where he studied with Paul de Man. Shortly after arriving in New Haven, he decided he wanted to leave the humanities and literature to study political science, this time at Harvard. Fukuyama wrote his dissertation there on the Middle Eastern foreign policy of the Soviet Union. At Harvard he met Samuel Huntington and became part of a group of friends that included Fareed Zakaria, Gideon Rose, and Eliot Cohen. Later he went to Washington, DC, to work on the policy planning staff of the State Department, where he met Lewis "Scooter" Libby.

In many ways Fukuyama does not seem American: he appears to be European in his thought and intellectual approach. Is he a typical American intellectual, or is he a European classical humanist? What role did his personal history and education play in his intellectual development?

A Classical Education

Your personal story is interesting because you did not start out as a political scientist; instead, it was classics and literature that first caught your attention. You have been called an idealist with a humanistic sensibility and a classical education. Is this description correct?

Yes, that's true. I've been really lucky in that I've had teachers who were really very influential and from whom I learned a lot. The first one was Allan Bloom, who was a political theorist and a follower of Leo Strauss. The very first course I took when I was a freshman at Cornell was a seminar on Plato's *Republic*, and Bloom is the one that persuaded me that I should be a classics major and learn Greek so I could read Plato and Aristotle in the original. It's what I then went on to do.

You told the *Guardian* that you inherited a first edition copy of Karl Marx's *Das Kapital* and that your mother listened to Beethoven.[1] What are the most valuable and formative experiences from your adolescence, growing up in postwar America?

My mother came to the United States in 1949. She grew up in Japan. She was born in 1917. Her father was a very prominent economist, Shiro Kawata, who had helped found the economics department at Kyoto University, which is one of the best universities in Japan. He was part of this generation that had been sent out during the Meiji Restoration to Europe. He learned German and went to Germany before World War I. There he bought the library of Werner Sombart, the social theorist. Marx's *Capital* came from Sombart's library. My grandfather actually donated the library to a university in Japan. So it's still there. In that period, Japan was modernizing and wanted to learn everything about the West. When I look back at my ancestors, they were all Westernized already. It's not as if I have any immediate ancestors who came out of a very different cultural tradition.

You feel close to them and these ideas from Europe.

Yes, they have followed me all my life.

All around us there are books. I ask if there are other books than *Das Kapital* that have left an imprint on his thinking. Fukuyama points to a shelf beside me where sociology classics are stacked closely together, and the names on the spines read Max Weber, Karl Marx, Ferdinand Tönnies.

I remember when I was young, my mother told me about Ferdinand Tönnies's concept of *Gemeinschaft and Gesellschaft.*[2] She studied a lot of European social theory, and so did my father because he got his degree in the sociology of religion. Actually, if you look on my shelf, you can see many books by Max Weber. I inherited them from my father, like that one right there, Weber's *Essays in Sociology.*

You virtually grew up with those books?

Yes, my mother was in the School of Social Work. She was aiming to do something more practical. But she also had a very Western education when she was in Japan because she went to a Christian university in Kyoto. Actually, it was a strange thing, and I think this is a complete accident: my grandmother on my father's side also converted to Christianity.

Which is not so common?

No, not at all.

They brought that with them coming to the United States?

Yes, my father became an ordained Protestant minister in the Congregational Church, a very progressive Protestant denomination that is now called the United Church of Christ. I remember that it was a source of friction between me and my father. Today I am not active in the Presbyterian church I belonged to.

No Ethnic Separateness

Fukuyama grew up in America when identity politics was not as strong as today. It was more common to think about oneself as American, not as having different ethnicities.

Why didn't you feel different?

Well, it's a little bit complicated because I grew up in New York City, which was very cosmopolitan and multicultural. I went to private schools because even back in the 1960s, the public schools were really not very good. Beginning in the 1960s, it became much more fashionable to retain your ethnic identity and not give that up so easily. It meant that you continued to speak or tried to learn the language of your ancestors and to stay within the community, but when I was young that was not so. We never took part in the Japanese community; it was not possible to really because in New York City such a community didn't really exist.

Did you ever face identity issues?

When I was twelve I moved to Pennsylvania. It was in the middle of this big agricultural area where half the students were the children of faculty members at Penn State; the other half were children of farmers. They actually kept us in separate academic tracks. We never saw the farmer kids in class.

Did you ever deal with them?

Well, it was interesting because you did get these racial things: the farmer kids would make fun of me for being Asian and that sort of thing. It was really different from New York City, where I never experienced racist comments, but I can illustrate my point by an anecdote from my family. There was a large Japanese American community in Los Angeles back then, unlike in New York City. Actually, I think my cousins' parents may have tried to send them to a Japanese-language school. Nonetheless, they were Americanized. None of that stuck at all. They tried, but it didn't work. In fact, my uncle was a social worker in a church that was in a very African American part of town, which then turned mostly Hispanic. His sons basically grew up in the inner city.

It's interesting because one of my cousins has become a Hollywood screenwriter. He wrote a couple of scripts for Goldie Hawn. I like telling the story because I'm really proud of what happened. He's a couple of years older than me. Late in life he decided that he was going to stop writing movie scripts and wanted to write a novel. He wrote a crime novel that is set in South Central Los Angeles, and the main character is a really smart Black private investigator. He'd never published a novel before, so he sent it to me and asked me to look at it and suggest where he might be able to get it published. I read it and thought it was just a great book because he grew up in that very violent poor community, and he understands the language and the characters. I told him that it is a really great book and sent it to my literary agent. She read it. She loved it. He got a book contract and has just published the fourth in his series of novels. He has also got a contract to turn his novel into a movie. That's not based on anything Japanese whatsoever. He actually knows how people in the inner city in Los Angeles talk and act and think.

It is clearly different in the United States today when it comes to identity and to what it is to be an American from the time you grew up.

Yes, when I was growing up, being American was to believe in the Constitution, the rule of law, and the idea that all people had equal rights. You could like watching baseball or football or whatever, and that's what they do in America. It was not about skin color. I see that in my own family. My grandfather on my father's side came from Japan in 1905. By the time my father grew up in the thirties and forties, already there was a shift toward a more open understanding of what it was to be an American. This did not prevent my family from being interned during World War II; my grandfather lost his business in Los Angeles, and my relatives spent the war in a relocation center in Colorado.

But my father's generation led a redress movement that eventually led to an official apology for the internment during the Reagan administration and payment of compensation to everyone who had been in camp. Eventually, Americans developed a civic identity. That's now under threat from those who would like to restore this old idea that Americans are basically white people. I expect in the long run that we're going to go back to the original idea of being an American. We have no choice. Our country is way too diverse today to go back to any understanding of being American related to race ethnicity.

Transcending Academic Disciplines

Fukuyama covers many academic fields in his writing. In that way, he resembles Enlightenment thinkers who followed ideas and not academic disciplines, as we tend to do today, at least in the Anglo-American tradition. A professor at the University of Chicago, Nathan Tarcov, once said the following about Fukuyama: "As a social scientist and policy person he was interested and knowledgeable about literary and aesthetic matters, which was a rare combination."[3]

Which academic discipline do you see yourself as part of today? And how do you see your contribution to a deeper understanding of society and politics?

Well, being interdisciplinary really is important because all of the different disciplines are built around methodologies. The tendency is that they get preoccupied with the methodology and not with the substance of what they are trying to study. That's true regardless of whether you're a historian or a political scientist or an economist or an anthropologist. They all have the incentives to do so. If you're an academic, you are to focus on the methodology and to show that you've mastered it, and that you can actually advance the methodology in your field. All the important insights about human societies are learned by combining things across different fields because human beings are so complex. The discipline I find the most profitable to study is some combination of sociology and anthropology, or maybe something like social anthropology, because some of the biggest insights I've had about how societies actually work and develop come from those areas of study, even if I had had no formal training in them. And it's funny because my father was a sociologist. When I was growing up, I said, I'm never going to become a sociologist like my father, and it turned out that I ended up one.

The Liberal Humanist and the Importance of Teaching History

The interesting question is how a liberal humanist intellectual can teach us something that is valuable and brings new perspectives and understanding. You have been asked how you would inculcate a sense of what 1989 meant—what we're fighting for and what we're fighting against—to a new generation that never experienced it. What can we do?

I believe that teaching history is necessary to every new generation. But often this is difficult, and it takes time to understand, for instance, what people experienced during World War I and why it was different from World War II. World War II was much more ideological, whereas World War I was the end of an era and much more hopeless and pointless.

Should history be an important part of the curriculum, or do we have other means of learning? You read a lot of literature in your youth and studied literature.

Yes, literature, novels, and films have given me many insights. When I was younger, and since I was a literature major and wanted to go to graduate school in comparative literature, I read everything. I liked all of the classics. I especially liked French literature: Stendhal, *Madame Bovary*, and all those classics. Of English literature, I read George Eliot, Charles Dickens, and all those people. Reading literature also helped me understand history and what it was like living during wars, which I had not experienced myself. A book that really struck me and made me realize the hopelessness of World War I was Erich Maria Remarque's *All Quiet on the Western Front*. Recently I took my students to see a film, *The Life of Others*, to share with them what it was like to live under the Stasi in East Germany before 1989.

* * *

The picture that emerges of Fukuyama is of a classical scholar, a humanist, and an academic who is preoccupied with understanding how politics and society work. He is the classical humanist who became more interested in understanding society even though he didn't want to become like his father when he was younger. He is the conservative bureaucrat who became a world-famous political scientist. He is an

American with a soft spot for European political thought. He is a proponent of interdisciplinarity and of intellectual curiosity.

Notes

1. "History's Pallbearer."
2. Ferdinand Tönnies was one of the best-known nineteenth-century German sociologists, whose main work was *Gemeinschaft und Gesellschaft*, from 1887.
3. "History's Pallbearer."

SEVEN

What Led Fukuyama to International Politics?

After earning his doctorate at Harvard, Fukuyama spent almost a decade getting to know the main political conflicts of the 1980s, alternately employed at the RAND Corporation and at the State Department. As a political appointee in the first Reagan administration, he joined the American delegation for the Egyptian-Israeli talks on Palestinian autonomy in 1981–82. When George H. W. Bush won the 1988 US presidential election, Fukuyama became a deputy director of policy planning under Secretary of State James Baker. At RAND he had also worked on the Soviet Union's foreign policy.

Deconstructive Nonsense

You were an undergraduate at Cornell before going to Paris to join the courses of Jacques Derrida and Roland Barthes, the French post-structuralists and deconstructivists. What did you find at Cornell and Telluride House?

I went to Cornell in the early 1970s just as French deconstructionism, structuralism, and postmodernism was hitting American campuses. I was introduced to Jacques Lacan, Jacques Derrida, Tzvetan Todorov, Julia Kristeva, and Michel Foucault, the latter three of whom visited Cornell and Telluride in this period. At the time it seemed extremely trendy and, well, European, something that homespun Americans would never be able to fully understand. Foucault, as I remember, spent the weekend with a bunch of young men he had somehow picked up. I remember Julia Kristeva telling me that there was a point to Stalinism.

It was just like a fashion wave. I was just curious to see this, the latest thing. We Americans didn't really understand this postmodernism/structuralism very well, but this was obviously the most exciting thing going on in philosophy at that time. I really didn't understand very much what the argument was, so I went to France and I read through Derrida's books.

Many years ago, you said that "perhaps when you're young you think that something must be profound just because it is difficult and you don't have the self-confidence to say, 'This is just nonsense.'"[1] I can freely admit that I share your view. What did you expect to learn before you left, and why did you return to the United States after just one semester? Did this experience influence your further professional and educational choices, and if so, how?

In Paris I went to this really ridiculous seminar by Roland Barthes. When he was younger, he wrote some really interesting books, like his book on photography. But in this seminar, he was writing, or he said he was writing, a dictionary. In the seminar he began with A, B, C, and then there was basically free associating. What do these letters make you think of: armée, bébé, café, etc., and we just went from one word to another. It just seemed very self-indulgent to me because he was a famous intellectual and could just say anything he wanted. These students would take notes on it and say, "Oh, that's very profound."

Obviously, you were disappointed, so you left.

It took a little bit longer because I had applied to the Yale Comparative Literature Department, which at that time was the leading postmodernist comparative literature department. Paul de Man was the big guru there. I actually took a couple of courses from De Man, but almost as soon as I got there, I decided I wasn't going to do it.

Do you think it was a waste, or did some of it give you something valuable?

I don't regret having done any of that.

I think that having a humanistic education is very important because, normally, when you start directly into something more technical, you don't go back to do the classics.

Yes, I think that's right. I have just a little anecdote about Friedrich Nietzsche that I came to think about, because I was in Sils-Maria, Switzerland, in November 2018. I saw where Nietzsche had gone in the summertime in the last few years of his life. When I was young, I was thinking of imitating Nietzsche, just in the sense that he studied classical philology and knew all those Greek authors just incredibly well. I thought that's what I wanted to be able to do. So when I made the shift out of this French structuralism, I thought I was going to go back to studying Greek and doing classics, but finally I decided that I wasn't going to do that. I decided instead that I would go into a contemporary discipline, political science.

But you haven't forgotten the Greek classics, because you are using them all the time.

Yes, that's true.

Before we leave the French structuralism, why did you get so angry? Was it the relativism implicit in their approach that upset you?

It was a kind of hypocrisy because it seemed to me that they still remained very much on the Left. If they were really consistent about their relativism, there's no reason why they should not choose fascism over socialism. At least I thought that Nietzsche was much more honest. He said if Christianity is dead then everything is permitted, and he asked why the stronger could not rule the weaker. It is provocative, but he thought through the consequences of relativism very clearly.

Most of the French intellectuals are Far Left. I'm really struggling to think of anyone who is moderate. It's not fashionable for a French intellectual to be in the middle somehow. Would you agree?

The only French intellectual who was remotely like that was Raymond Aron. Another classical liberal may be François Furet, a historian of the French Revolution, but hardly anyone was liberal. There were really no French liberals at that time.[2]

The Desire to Do Something Down-to-Earth

Fukuyama did not become a professor of comparative literature. He changed direction to political theory and became a think tank analyst and a bureaucrat.

Many famous professors crossed your educational path—would you like to tell me whether and how they influenced the choices you made?

One who's pretty influential is Harvey Mansfield, who is a political theorist at Harvard. I studied with him.

You chose Harvard to study with him?

Yes, because at that point if you wanted to do political theory in that tradition, you either went to Toronto to study with Bloom, who had moved there, or you went to Harvard to study with Mansfield. I just chose to go to Harvard. He was an influential teacher, but then I decided I wasn't going to do theory. I wanted to do contemporary international relations. In a way, it was a little bit of a reaction to all of the French theory that I'd been doing, and I kind of wanted to do the opposite. I wanted to do something really down-to-earth, the real thing.

Was it a relief to leave abstract academic ideas, or did you miss it?

After making the switch to more policy-oriented studies, I never looked back. I started reading the newspapers for the first time in my life and felt that the frame of the Cold War provided some grounding for right and wrong. I remember going into the office of Geoffrey Hartman, one of the famous comparative literature professors at Yale at that time, and telling him I wanted out of his department, and he said, "Yes, I can see you're clutching the *New York Times* and that your mind is elsewhere." In the late 1970s I published my first article in *Commentary*, which was then the bible of the group that would become known as neoconservatives. I wrote an article on Soviet incursions in the Middle East and sent it to Norman Podhoretz "over the transom." To everyone's surprise, he accepted it right away, and I was paid five hundred dollars, the first money I ever earned as a writer. I went out and spent it immediately on a Nikon camera.

The Fall of the Wall

Tell me your story from after your graduate studies in political science at Harvard.

I wrote my dissertation on Soviet foreign policy in the Middle East. I got my PhD in 1981. The next decade or so I was either working in the State Department or at RAND Corporation, a think tank in Santa Monica, California. I concentrated mostly on Middle Eastern things but also on the Soviet Union. When George H. W. Bush was president, in 1989–90, I was again working on Soviet affairs. I went to the Soviet Union maybe four or five times during the 1980s, and that's the time when I was trying to learn Russian. It was really interesting being there. It was a police state, but it was also evident that it was a funny police state because nobody actually seemed to believe in the ideology, and everybody was very cynical about it. We had a lot of staged meetings. At that point they had the Institute for US and Canadian Studies. You could go there, and these people were not real scholars. They were just propagandists. You would have these seemingly formal arguments, and then you would go and have a drink, and they would admit that they were not scholars. This was how it was really working.

We embark on a detailed description of Fukuyama's months in Europe in 1989.

I had been following all of these reports from people coming out of East Germany. The crisis started more than a year before the actual fall of the Berlin Wall. I had a number of friends who were very close to developments in Eastern Europe and in the Soviet Union, and they kept saying, "You don't understand what's happening." It turned out they were right; things were really moving very quickly there. In mid-1989 I went with George H. W. Bush, who spoke in Gdańsk alongside Lech Walesa. At the same time, you had this civil society movement in Hungary, and you had the Solidarity movement in Poland. It looked like both of those states were going to liberalize. I said to myself, it doesn't make any sense that all these countries around East Germany are going to liberalize, and East Germany is going to remain this bastion of Stalinism.

So, what did you decide to do?

I wrote a memo to Secretary James Baker through my boss, Dennis Ross, saying that we should start thinking about German unification because that was the logic of all these developments. I remember at the time that, the more that you knew about Germany—the more you were an expert on Germany—the less you thought reunification was possible. All the German experts in the State Department said that it was ridiculous, that it was not going to happen, and we can't think about it. This continued right up until the end. In late October of 1989 we were at a NATO planning meeting in the South of France. The German representative said Germany would never unify in his lifetime. After the meeting, I went on to East Berlin and talked to a lot of the American diplomats in East Germany. This was like the first few days of November 1989.

You were almost there?

Yes, and then they set me up in meetings with these East German Communist Party members, and they said they—and not the liberal members of civil society—were going to be the future of Germany. But within a week the wall came down.

Choosing Intellectual Liberty over Bureaucratic Power

Everyone who lived through 1989 has a sense of that political change. I told Fukuyama that I spent the summer of 1989 going by car through Eastern Europe, seeing communism, fences, talking to students, and finding the first McDonalds in Budapest with an enormous queue. It left an impression on me that I will never forget, and, as the above account shows, also on Fukuyama.

During the summer of 1989 Fukuyama published the article "The End of History?" in the conservative journal *National Interest*. Nobody thought it was going to get any attention, least of all Fukuyama. But it did. All the large newspapers, from the *Washington Post* to the *Wall Street Journal*, and magazines from *Time* to *Newsweek* picked it up. It was a sensation. The state bureaucrat was to change his career and eventually become a world-famous academic.

In the preface of your book *Trust*, you write that Alexandre Kojève had concluded Georg Hegel was right in declaring that history had ended. Kojève therefore decided he had no further work to do as a philosopher and decided to be a full-time bureaucrat, which he was until he died. You add that this might have been the path you could have taken yourself, as you had declared the end of history, but you chose otherwise. Why?

That's just a personal choice. I worked as a bureaucrat twice in the State Department and I really didn't like it that much. And so I figured, why? I mean, a lot of my friends—like Paul Wolfowitz or Scooter Libby—went on to become pretty powerful bureaucrats, and it got them into a lot of trouble because you end up actually exercising real power, and if you don't make the right decisions, you can do a lot of damage.

In 2000 you started working as a professor at the Paul Nitze School of Advanced International Studies (SAIS) in Washington. What was your role in the Pentagon and White House workshops before the Iraq invasion?

In the year prior to the invasion of Iraq, the late Andrew Marshall, who was the long-standing director of the Pentagon's Office of Net Assessment, commissioned an "Autumn Study" in which he asked four teams to consider responses to the September 11 attack. I was the leader of one of these teams, which included my colleagues Roger Leeds and Tom Keaney from SAIS and Barbara Haig from the National Endowment for Democracy. We consulted a range of outside experts, including Sam Huntington, Larry Diamond, Fareed Zakaria, Michael Ignatieff, and Steve Hosmer, and collected a bibliography of materials on radical Islam, nation-building, and other subjects. The four teams briefed Marshall in January 2003. After presenting a threat assessment in our report, we argued that "the underlying problem ultimately can be solved only by attention to the political dimension" and that "the political dimension is not an afterthought but the core of the strategy." I don't know whether Paul Wolfowitz ever saw any of these briefings.

Did this influence your choice to work on state-building and on developing countries in the next decade?

Yes, this is the moment when I first started thinking systematically about the problem of state-building and nation-building. This led to my book *State-Building: Governance and World Order in the 21st Century*, based on the Messenger Lectures I was asked to give at Cornell in 2003. I was heavily involved in policy discussions swirling around Washington at that time about what had gone wrong with the Iraq invasion, and why the US government was so unprepared for doing state building. I also published an edited volume, *Nation-Building: Beyond Afghanistan and Iraq*, that was the consequence of a conference we held on this subject at SAIS. Eventually this would lead to my Political Order series: I began to realize that we political scientists had taken the state for granted and had little idea about how states came into existence and were eventually built.

James Thomson, a previous president and chief executive officer at RAND, said to the *Guardian* that he remembered you as being someone who "got into subjects that other people hadn't thought about." Did you?

One of the big problems with the tenure process in American universities is that it incentivizes young academics to specialize in an extremely narrow subject area and to focus on the fashionable cutting-edge methodology in their field. I avoided this in two ways; first, by starting my career at RAND, which didn't have tenure and was committed to interdisciplinary research, and, second, by writing *The End of History and the Last Man*. Once I published that book, I was freed to write whatever I wanted outside of an academic institution. I remember when Erwin Glikes, my first publisher, came to me after *The End of History* had become a best seller and asked what I would like to write next. I thought to myself, this is great, I can study whatever I want to. I had always been interested in the relationship of culture to economic growth—a topic I knew next to nothing about—so I decided to focus on that as my next project. This led to my second book, *Trust: The Social Virtues and the Creation of Prosperity*, which in certain ways was even more successful than *The End of History*. Among other things, it led to my getting my first academic position as Hirst Professor of Public Policy at George Mason University, which came with an endowed chair and tenure. So, I managed to avoid the tenure-track trap altogether.

You also got praise from people who would have liked your continuing to work for the government.[3] But you wanted intellectual freedom.

Intellectual freedom is only part of it. Yes, I can pretty much say whatever I want as an academic, whereas in the government you are always speaking on behalf of your political principal. Today that has become very problematic when your principal is a corrupt incompetent who is asking you to do things that likely violate the Constitution. But government service also gives you huge power that can be misused. My friends in the Bush administration made, I believe, disastrous choices with regard to the Iraq War, and I am very glad I don't have to live with those consequences.

You are obviously very interested in politics, and many people with strong political views interact with you when you publish books, articles, and columns. But you are an academic, not a politician. Am I correct in saying that ideas, arguments, and intellectual curiosity matter more to you than "day-to-day" politics?

Both ideas and activism matter, but I'm much better suited to dealing with the former. Ideas are absorbed by activists and political leaders and become embedded in the way they see the world. The rise of the Chicago school in economics provided a sophisticated justification for the dramatic shift away from states and toward markets that took place following the rise of Reagan and Thatcher in the 1980s. Those ideas hugely influenced two generations of policymakers, for example, in the realm of antitrust. If we are going to recover from the excesses of "neo-liberalism" we are going to have to replace that paradigm with something else, and that's the job of thinkers rather than doers.

You write and publish extensively in both academic journals and in political newspapers and magazines. You were, for instance, one of the founders of *American Interest*. What does intellectual freedom mean to you?

I think right now there are all sorts of issues of intellectual freedom on university campuses, not outside the university. I think the problem in a modern liberal society is not having overt constraints on intellectual freedom but that there are more informal ones where, because of social pressures and because you are part of a peer group, you don't want to say things or confront certain problems. That was an issue breaking with all my neoconservative friends, because they were my friends, and they had taken very strong positions on things. As a result, a number of them stopped speaking to me or got really angry with things I was saying about them and so forth. That makes things hard, and I think that's the problem with intellectual freedom.

The invasion of Iraq and American foreign policy more generally ended the friendship with the neoconservatives. In 2006, you published *America at the Crossroads: Democracy, Power, and the Neoconservative Legacy*. In short, how do you explain the decision to break with the neoconservative movement?

It wasn't really a movement, more like-minded intellectuals who wrote for journals like the *Public Interest* or *Commentary*. Bill Kristol shifted the focus of some neoconservatives from a focus on ideas to policy advocacy after September 11, but there was by no means broad agreement with this. As I argued in *America at the Crossroads*, the notion that American power could be used to reshape the Middle East was at complete variance with neoconservative arguments about the limits of state power to change outcomes in the context of US domestic policy.

In an interview after the publication of *America at the Crossroads* you were asked if "there are no shortcuts to the end of history"—that is, to liberalism and democracy. And you answered, "If Iraq has taught us anything, it is that there are no shortcuts."[4] Do you believe that the United States understands this?

I think the United States has learned this, perhaps a bit too well. Both Obama and Trump have abjured military intervention in the Middle East, and both have tried to withdraw the United States from commitments there.

The remark about shortcuts refers to something the scholar Ken Jowitt once said to the effect that if I was the Karl Marx of democracy, then Bill Kristol was the Vladimir Lenin. That is, my view was that there would be a long, slow evolution in the direction of liberal democracy, driven by technology, economic change, and other structural factors. Kristol and his fellow neoconservatives, by contrast, believed that you could use military power to speed up this process. But in the end, I think our experience has shown that this shortcut does not exist, just as Lenin's did not.

What are your relations with these neoconservative friends today?

They are Republicans, but it turns out that many of my old neoconservative friends whom I broke with over the Iraq War have been turned into Never Trumpers and broke with the Republican Party. They've been willing to completely alienate all their old Republican colleagues and suffer political exile. This is something I learned. When you break up with people on politics, it has a lot of personal consequences. You grow up in a circle of friends, and then you take a position and all of a sudden, they don't like you anymore. They don't invite you over for dinner. It happened to me, and it's tough to go through.

You have been employed at different universities and are now at Stanford. Why did you come here?

I was invited by Larry Diamond and Mike McFaul, who were old friends of mine, and I had wanted to move back to California at some point. I was tired of being in Washington. Obviously, the weather is nicer here, and it's a nice place to be. I have valuable colleagues here. But, of course, the intellectual side is the most important thing, even if the way you live is also important.

* * *

Fukuyama is currently living in Palo Alto, California, and is employed at Stanford University, where he directs the Center on Democracy, Development and the Rule of Law.

Notes

1. "History's Pallbearer."
2. Raymond Aron (1905–83) was a French philosopher and sociologist who wrote critically about Marxism in a book from 1955, *The Opium of the Intellectuals*. François Furet (1927–97) was a French historian who challenged the Marxist interpretation of the French Revolution.
3. See "History's Pallbearer."
4. "There Are No Shortcuts to 'the End of History.'"

EIGHT

What Is the End of History?

If someone says "the end of history," it is almost sure to be a reference to Fukuyama. Likewise if someone says "getting to Denmark." The popular understanding of Fukuyama is that he is the one who claimed that liberal democracy was the end of history and that Denmark was a metaphor for a successful society. It is important to understand *The End of History* to trace the development in Fukuyama's ideas and thoughts. It is at first sight the most optimistic book he has written, but a closer look shows a more pessimistic perception of the future. Furthermore, as we will discover, it is probably one of the most misinterpreted books. But it is with books as it is with children; they live their own life—often completely independent of despairing parents' wishes and intentions.

A Defense of the Idea of Liberal Democracy

The article "The End of History?" was published in 1989. What was your main message?

For more than a hundred years, most progressive intellectuals thought the end of history was going to lead to communism. That was the end of history for Karl Marx. Marx borrowed the concept of the end of history from Hegel. In the year prior to 1988–89 I began to think that it didn't look like we're going to get to the Marxist end of history but, rather, that we were going toward something more like the Hegelian end of history, which would be a liberal state or a liberal democracy tied to a market economy. And that was really the argument I was making. Then it was misunderstood.

I used the end of history in the Hegelian, Marxist sense. A contemporary synonym for history in this sense would be "development" or "modernization." The question of the end of history was not the stopping of history. It was the question of where modernization was leading.

What made you write the article, and how did you come up with the idea?

I was working at the RAND Corporation. We were a dozen people who specialized in the Soviet Union, mostly on foreign policy and security issues. But we increasingly started to look at Soviet domestic policy because that seemed to be changing very rapidly. And at one point I read a Gorbachev speech. This is probably in 1987 or so, where he said that the essence of socialism is competition. I thought this was a big development. The friends of mine who studied political theory knew about the "end of history." This wasn't a new phrase. Everybody in that circle knew that Hegel and Kojève had used it. So I called one of my friends and said, "If Gorbachev is saying this, then this is the end of history." I guess that's where the idea originated. I was asked by Allan Bloom and Nathan Tarcov to give a lecture at the University of Chicago. The lecture series was on the decline of the West—with a question mark. They asked me to speak, and I said, "Well, I'm going to speak, but it's not going to be about the decline. It's going to be about the victory of the West." They said, "Okay, go ahead."

We often hear you mention the Russian-born philosopher Alexandre Kojève as an inspiration. How did you hear about Kojève? What is it that he sees in Hegel that you find interesting?

Well, Kojève was probably the most famous intellectual in the interwar period in France. He had a very influential seminar on the reading of Hegel. His notes were published as a book, *Introduction à la lecture de Hegel.* Raymond Queneau, Jean-Paul Sartre, Raymond Aron, there were many postwar French intellectuals who were part of that seminar. Kojève abstracted out of Hegel's *Phenomenology of Spirit* the idea that history had actually ended concretely with the French Revolution, with the ideas of liberty and equality being universalized. What he said was "It's achieved." But the victory had taken place only in the metropolitan areas, primarily on the level of ideas. In the periphery it still hadn't penetrated, but it was going to do that. It struck me that Kojève was right that we hadn't gone beyond the liberal republic at the French Revolution in terms of a normative understanding of a just social order. We tried all sorts of alternatives of fascism and communism, and none of those really worked very well.

The idea that history in reality is characterized by incidents, crises, and developments is not the same as the concept of history;—the idea of a dialectical development that gradually diminishes contradictions in political order. The second part of *The End of History* is actually quite gloomy.

The "last man" sections of *The End of History* are all about what could go wrong in a successful liberal democracy. The problem is the fact that peace and prosperity will not ultimately be satisfying to many people who will continue to seek recognition and community. For this reason I said very clearly back then that neither nationalism nor religion would disappear from world politics, but few people remember that now.

Right-Wing Criticism as the Most Dangerous Threat to Liberal Democracy

In 1995 you wrote the article "Reflections on *The End of History,* Five Years On," where your main point is

> [My critics] fundamentally miss the point of the phrase, "the end of history." The latter is not a statement about the *is*, but about the *ought*: for a variety of *theoretical* reasons, liberal democracy and free markets constitute the best regime, or more precisely the best of the available alternative ways of organizing human societies (or again, if one prefers Churchill's formulation, the least bad way of doing so). It most fully (though not completely) satisfies the most basic human longings, and therefore can be expected to be more universal and more durable than other regimes or other principles of political organization. It does not *completely* satisfy them, however, which means that the resolution of the historical problem cannot be brought to a close.
>
> This is a normative, not an empirical statement.[1]

Can you comment on the attacks from the Left?

The most significant criticism isn't on the Left because most people on the Left had at that point given up on communism. Nobody was willing to argue that there's a higher stage where we're going to nationalize all private property and have a centralized Leninist state. There's a species of criticism that says you still have these big contradictions in capitalism, and that you need to somehow move to a different economic system, but I've never really understood what that alternative is other than greater regulation of the capitalist system and stronger social protections. You can have a little bit more, you can have a little bit less, but you're still basically within a market economy. The only alternative is getting to the point where you start seriously trying to abolish private property, and not very many people are willing to go that far except in certain limited sectors.

What is the most plausible and dangerous critique of your argument today?

Well, there's a couple of different kinds, but the one that may be the most dangerous is from the Right. This is something that's interesting to watch, because the Right is slowly developing a view that the problem really is with liberalism, that you don't want an open and completely tolerant society. The reason is that since you have societies that are built around national identities, they want to preserve those identities and therefore they don't want to accept gay marriage and so forth. They believe they have a right not to. That's what's fueling a lot of these populist movements, and the Russians are at the center of this. Putin really didn't start with his position. He adopted it because it justified what he was doing. The Russians are now beginning to say, "Yes, there's this alternative that's based on traditional Christian values, and we don't want a liberal society that's decadent and promoting all sorts of things." It's the liberal part they are objecting to.

A Thesis to Agree with and to Misunderstand

In the early 2000s newspaper headlines said that 9/11 was "The End of Fukuyama" and that it was Huntington's thesis about the clash of civilizations that had won. Amitai Etzioni pointed out that "Fukuyama is one of the few enduring public intellectuals. They are often media stars who are eaten up and spat out after their 15 minutes. But he has lasted."[2] Paul Sagar at Kings College wrote an article about Fukuyama in 2017. According to Sagar, *The End of History* is probably the most misunderstood book after World War II.[3] The thesis still meets with reactions.

How was it to experience being misread and misunderstood?

Well, in all of the debates I have been in ever since I wrote that book, I've been trying to move on to discussions that I thought were more important than rehashing silly misunderstandings of my argument. I had to go over the same ground again and again. I'm not sure that these debates were terribly productive.

I agree, but why do you think your critics reacted like that? You certainly found a nerve. Can you elaborate, what were the arguments, and why do you think you got these reactions?

One source of hostility was related to American foreign and economic policies. Especially at the time of the Iraq War, a lot of people misunderstood me. I think the biggest mistake that I find really annoying was that they said that I was promoting a particular American neoliberal model in economics and a neoconservative one in foreign policy. This was never true. Right from the beginning I said that the European Union would represent more of the true end of history than the United States.

In your "Reflections on *The End of History*, Five Years On" you say that we cannot be too optimistic about the future, even if we think that liberal democracy is a well-functioning political order. Even if I can guess the answer, will there ever be an "End of"?

I think it can as a destination. It's still a question whether, in reality, we can actually come there. We have to strive for it.

The End of History **is a normative statement, not an empirical condition. History never stopped after 1989; all countries didn't become liberal democracies. Unrest, conflict, and wars happen all the time—in Bosnia, in Iraq, in Syria, in financial markets. In 2018 Yascha Mounk published *People*** *vs. Democracy: Why Our Freedom Is in Danger and How to Save It*, and in January 2020 he wrote a review in the *Journal of Democracy* that he titled "The End of History Revisited."[4] What does he say, thirty years after the publication of your book?

Yascha Mounk and I agree that it has become fashionable to announce the end of the end of history. I think he is right when he points out that people would want to keep universal recognition and respect in a democracy and not wish for an authoritarian political system. So far no autocratic regime has been able to fulfill the same recognition that democracies do, and until they do, my thesis holds on this score. But of course, things might change. Democracies have to provide well-functioning societies, and they have to sustain attempts to be overthrown by forces that will replace democracy with an authoritarian system. If democracies fail, my thesis will not hold anymore.

The basic question is, What happens when countries modernize? Do they become China, Iran, or Saudi Arabia?

No, as I once told a Danish interviewer, they become—or at least they strive to become—like Denmark.[5]

* * *

If this is where we are heading, how do we get to Denmark? And why should we go there? The end of history thesis is about liberal democracies and the idea that the ideological struggle between political systems had come to an end in a Hegelian sense. As Fukuyama wrote in the article "The End of History?" from 1989, "But at the end of history it is not necessary that all societies become successful liberal societies, merely that they end their ideological pretensions of representing different and higher forms of human society."[6] The functioning of liberal democracies has preoccupied Fukuyama ever since, and especially what it takes to make democracies work properly. This brings us to Denmark as an example of a well-functioning democracy with a trustworthy state and a meritocratic bureaucracy. State building was not the core issue in *The End of History*, but it has become increasingly important to Fukuyama over the years.

Notes

1. Fukuyama, "Reflections on *The End of History*, Five Years On," 201; see also Fukuyama, "Reflections on *The End of History* Five Years Later," 27.

2. "History's Pallbearer."

3. Sagar, "Last Hollow Laugh."

4. Mounk, "End of History Revisited."

5. "Fukuyama: Populismen peger paa ægte problemer, man har forkerte svar."

6. Fukuyama, "End of History?," 12.

NINE

Why Do We Go to Denmark?

In *The Federalist Papers: No. 70*, Alexander Hamilton wrote the following about state capacity: "A feeble execution is but another phrase for a bad execution; and a government ill executed, whatever it may be in theory, must be, in practice, a bad government." State building has been a preoccupation of Fukuyama's for a long time. *State-Building: Governance and World Order in the 21st Century* was published in 2004, and he has returned to the theme consistently, following up with *The Origins of Political Order: From Prehuman Times to the French Revolution* in 2011 and *Political Order and Political Decay: From the Industrial Revolution to the Globalization of Democracy* in 2014. There he argues that the lack of state building and state capacity is a main reason for weak political order. The two volumes of *Political Order* cover the whole globe, from Europe and the United States to China, Africa, and Latin America.

To a Scandinavian, it is flattering to be held up as a symbol of a good society, but Denmark is not an ideal, happy place for everyone. Fukuyama's thesis about Denmark must be seen through the lens of someone who wants to understand how a state becomes well-functioning and democratic and, most importantly, how state capacity and execution must operate within a strong rule of law.

State Capacity Is Important

Let's start with what happened in Russia after communism. What did failures in the 1990s have to do with the understanding of the state and its capacity?

The biggest mistake made by American policy advisers was to press for rapid liberalizing reforms, without adequate consideration of what would happen in the absence of a strong and legitimate state to oversee this process. There was a belief that markets would fill in the vacuum left by the collapsing Soviet state and that free markets would form spontaneously. In hindsight countries that transitioned from centralized planning more slowly did better.

A small but significant book, *State-Building*, that you wrote in 2004 is interesting because it discusses issues that have been neglected when describing liberal democracies. Much has been said about democracy but not about its "structure" and state building. Could you tell me what state building is and why you chose to dedicate a book to the topic?

After September 11, the United States invaded Afghanistan and Iraq. They thought, just get rid of Saddam Hussein and people were going to be democratic, and we can withdraw. And, literally, they were planning to withdraw six months after the invasion and spent no time thinking about how to create institutions. The image they had in their heads was the scene from *The Wizard of Oz*, where the Wicked Witch of the West dies and the Munchkins suddenly rise up in joyous celebration.

Americans discovered they had to build states in both countries because the states had collapsed after the invasions. Americans take the state for granted even though they don't like it. They actually didn't think that state building was important, and they didn't think about it as a requirement for what they would have to do after these invasions. All of a sudden they found themselves struggling. How do you create a police force or a finance ministry or a health program when it doesn't exist, or exists in a highly dysfunctional form? We ended up in these big state-building exercises in both Iraq and Afghanistan without a handbook, without even the most rudimentary knowledge about how you create a state in a situation where you've got this chaotic state of nature.

The reason the United States made this mistake dates back to 1989 because, in 1989, nobody expected the Soviet Union to collapse or the Berlin Wall to come down the way it did. There was very little violence all across Eastern Europe: Hungary, Poland, the Czech Republic, the Baltic states—all these countries made a relatively easy transition to functioning democracies. It was kind of a miracle that these countries turned out to be pretty decent democracies, at least for the first couple of decades. The lesson that some of my friends drew from that experience was that all you needed to do was get rid of the bad dictator and these natural processes would take over, and you would get a functioning democracy at the other end. And, unfortunately, they tried to put that in practice in Afghanistan and Iraq. The Republican policymakers who were in charge had last been in power at the time of the collapse of communism; they missed the Balkans and Rwanda and all the messy Third World interventions in between. One of the things that's been learned today certainly is a great deal more caution about these kinds of interventions. The United States is not going to rush into another Iraq or Afghanistan any time soon.

It would be interesting to know what exactly matters and why.

It's difficult to get things working without having adequate state capacity. The important thing is a high-quality state if you are going to be rich and stable. If you don't have a modern state, it doesn't matter whether it's large or small. You're not going to be happy. We're seeing the importance of such a state in the current COVID-19 crisis.

What do you think is the most valuable thing the state could do to enhance economic growth?

The core functions of the state are to provide certain public goods: defense, law enforcement, basic things like control over fiscal policy, and certain basic social services—infrastructure, health, and education. I don't know if there's a particular priority among those things, other than the need for basic citizen security. It depends on the situation of the state. Obviously, if you're Israel or South Korea, the external defense function is going to be a lot more important. But the precondition is doing those competently, as the precondition for any other thing you might want, like economic growth, or democracy, or observation of human rights, and so forth.

It would be interesting to hear your thoughts on the United States and on your impressions about Scandinavia.

I think Americans would never like a really large state like you have in Scandinavia.

And I don't think Scandinavians would ever like a kind of minimalist state. So what you're saying is that you have to base state building in the citizens' ideas about what the state should be.

Yes.

Another important aspect is the ability of the political system to solve conflicts and to compromise. You have said that "democratic political systems are not supposed to end conflict; they are supposed to peacefully resolve and lessen conflicts through agreed upon rules."[1] Can you explain this ability to solve conflict as a key factor in what you call state capacity?

The reasons you want institutions and rules is to provide channels for resolving conflicts that don't devolve into violence. That's why the state exists; it's really what the state can generate. It is an instrument for controlling violence, and one of the ways you do that is by shifting the locus of conflict from the streets into a parliament where you can argue and deliberate rather than fighting things out.

The modern state was really the topic of both of my books on political order. And that's the area that I really neglected when I was writing *The End of History and the Last Man*. It's easy to assume that a state will exist. If you live in a rich country, the police will come when you call them. Basically, you pay taxes and you get something back for them. I have spent quite a long time looking at the problems of developing countries, and you cannot take this for granted in India, for instance. If laws get violated, you can't be certain that someone is going to come to your rescue, because the state has very weak enforcement capability. If you're a factory owner and you dump pollutants into the river, nothing happens to you because you don't have a state that enforces law.

Denmark Is a Metaphor for Political Order

Fukuyama has written 1,300 pages on the origins of political order and about the importance of a well-functioning state. In other words, he has thought a lot about how to "get to Denmark." It is clear that economic and scientific realities influence political development, but is it also the case that liberal democracy presupposes economic growth, scientific development, and modernization?

The thesis of the Political Order books is simple enough, but the books are full of nuances. You underline the power and capacity of the state, the rule of law, and accountable democracy. And you point out the importance of order or sequencing. You said jokingly in a lecture in Oslo in 2015 that you had written *The Origins of Political Order* in order to find out which ways lead to Denmark or, for that matter, Norway. Did you?

Well, I had a visiting professorship at Aarhus University for three years.

You were there between 2009 and 2012, and *The Origins of Political Order* was published in 2011. Denmark must have left a good impression on you. Why did you choose Denmark?

Most people who like Denmark—Bernie Sanders, for example—like it because of social democracy, but that was never my intention. "Getting to Denmark" had to do with the absence of corruption and having a modern state, which is much harder to get to than just having a big state that provides welfare benefits to people. The big countries of Latin America all tried to create welfare states and failed miserably. That was really the reason for my interest. The phrase "getting to Denmark" wasn't mine. Michael Woolcock and Lant Pritchett at the Kennedy School and the World Bank had written this article called "Getting to Denmark."[2] It was a little bit of an inside joke in development circles. They had the notion that there was a template for getting to Denmark in all these poor countries, and that was not very realistic.

It's a good phrase though. You have explained "getting to Denmark" by saying that "Denmark" stands for a country with well-functioning state institutions. But you also add a question. Even if we know how "Denmark" works and how it came to be, can we successfully transfer some useful knowledge to other countries that may be very different culturally and historically from Denmark as it actually exists?

Yes, everybody who was working on governance issues at the World Bank at that time kind of implicitly had this model that you wanted to take Tanzania or Myanmar or Somalia and turn it into some version of Denmark. It was very hard for people to admit that this would just never happen.

You went to Denmark; did you stay there or live there?

I kept going there for two to three weeks at a time over a three-year period, and I gave a lot of papers at conferences and so forth.

What do you think was the most valuable insight you gained from your time there?

I saw that Danish universities are a lot like American ones because they're selective. In France or Germany or in the Netherlands, they have admissions policies where everybody gets in, and then they have to flunk out two-thirds of the students because they can't handle the work. There's very little selectivity. Danish universities are much more like American academic institutions. They're much more selective about the quality of their students. I thought the quality of the professors was really good in political science. America has gone over to quantitative political science to such an extent that many professors have ceased talking about the real world. There was a certain point where Denmark was getting a little bit like this, but I think the Danes were much more anchored in a more interesting older tradition of studying politics.

Did you learn something that you have been able to use afterward?

One thing was just watching the way that Danish politics worked, because it's built on such a foundation of social consensus. I think consensus seeking is also a weakness because of immigration and other pressures. Whether Denmark can maintain that consensus over the long run is an interesting question. But there is also something cultural. There was a really interesting conference at Aarhus on national identity when I was there. I wrote a paper that ended up as a chapter in my book about the United States in the development of American national identity.[3] I just remembered several of the discussions in that conference. There was an American woman who was married to a Dane, and she'd been living in Denmark for the last ten years or so, and she said, "I still don't feel like I'm remotely accepted in this country because they have all these little traditions that Danes grew up with—about what kind of fish you eat with what meal and all these little rituals—and if you don't know them you're treated as an outsider." It's just interesting having little insights like that about how it works.

The Protestant Influence on the Strong Danish State

Fukuyama wrote three articles about Luther to commemorate the five hundredth anniversary of the Reformation in 2017. Two of them concerned the importance of Luther when it comes to the emergence of modern states and the influence of the Reformation on modern liberalism.

How important was Lutheran and Calvinist Protestantism for the emergence of the modern state?

In northern Europe, you have Luther, and you have John Calvin as well. The two wings of the Reformation had different effects that were both important to modernization. The Lutheran influence was important in terms of strengthening the state and centralizing its power. Princes all over Europe used the Reformation as an excuse to seize the properties of the Catholic Church, which were incorporated into state. The Lutherans also felt it was important for people to read the Bible and so encouraged mass literacy. The Calvinist wing was really important in getting rid of corruption because there is a kind of austere personal morality that was cultivated in the Calvinist tradition, which was important in the founding of modern bureaucracies in the Netherlands, in Prussia, in England, and in the United States.

I think in the end that corruption is a very natural thing. You want to help your friends, and you want to help your family. This idea that you should be impersonal and not steal on behalf of your friends or your family doesn't occur to anyone unless they're forced to do it. Calvinism imposed a kind of morality on its believers that was conducive to a strict order, in which you could tell bureaucrats that this is really wrong. Unless you internalize those rules, no amount of external surveillance is going to make people really honest.

What do you consider to be the most original thoughts that you present in these two large volumes of political order?

I don't know if it's an original thought, but the single message that I extract from all this history is that the most helpful thing for modernization and development is having a modern state but also that a modern state is one of the hardest institutions to create. The modern state is really more important than people thought.

* * *

Most people have no idea how their countries became liberal democracies, least of all the Danes. No other country can copy the Danes' history, culture, and political system, but lessons can be learned. Adam Przeworski and Fernando Limongi claimed in an article called "Modernization: Theories and Facts" from 1997 that if a country reached the income per capita of Argentina in 1975, $6,055, and they succeeded in changing government through fair and free elections a few times, they would stay democratic. The next question is, Does it matter when and how political order is established?

Notes

1. Fukuyama, *Political Order and Political Decay*, 490.

2. Lant Pritchett and Michael Woolcock first asked "the best way to get to 'Denmark'" in their article "Solutions When the Solution Is the Problem."

3. Fukuyama, *Political Order and Political Decay*, chapter 12, "Nation Building."

TEN

How Do We Build Liberal Democracies?

Fukuyama bases his analyses on political, social, religious, and intellectual history. First, he examines the development of the rule of law. Second, he traces the origins of the state and the value and importance of meritocratic bureaucracies. This latter project does not exclusively involve European intellectual history; the Chinese had a meritocratic bureaucracy much earlier. The United States and Europe are different when it comes to the historical development of liberal democracy. In France and Germany, the rule of law came first, then the modern state with bureaucracy, and, finally, democratization. In the United States, the English common law came first, then democracy, and, finally, the development of a modern bureaucracy.

Samuel Huntington's hypothesis in *Political Order in Changing Societies* from 1968 was that order—meaning institutions and the rule of law—came first and then economic development. In *Political Order and Political Decay* Fukuyama writes that "Huntington's work was critical in making people understand that political development was a separate process from economic and social growth, and that before a polity could be democratic, it had to provide basic order. For all of the differences between Huntington's book and my own in form and substance, I come to the same basic conclusions that he did."[1] It took Europe several centuries to establish political order. The issue for many developing countries today is how to do many things at the same time.

Ideas and Social Structures Matter

I have spent a lot of time reading your historical works, and I have been trying to understand the importance of the building blocks of liberal

democracy and their sequencing over time. As an intellectual historian, I am curious about the interaction and reciprocal influence between ideas and historical development. Can you tell me about the sequencing of the different building blocks of liberal democracy and its historical importance? And how do you see this reciprocal influence between ideas and historical development?

I don't think there's a systematic way that I understand any of this, but it just seems to me that causality clearly works in both directions. Certain ideas are taken up at a certain period because the material conditions make them more plausible, but that can't be the whole explanation. Sometimes you have the same material conditions for hundreds of years, and then all of a sudden things change because someone came up with a different kind of way of conceptualizing things. This is something that Allan Bloom pointed out a long time ago, which I think was right. There's a fundamental fight between Marx and Weber in terms of what has priority, material conditions or ideas. Karl Marx said that religion is the opium of the people, and it's simply a kind of a fairy tale that the capitalists tell in order to make the workers docile and so forth. Weber said that causality works exactly the opposite way, that capitalism itself could not have arisen apart from certain ideas that were carried in Protestantism.

Somewhere in his book on the sociological method, Emile Durkheim argues that economists say that people are motivated by the piece rate—you'll work more if you're paid by every output that you do—but in certain societies people work until they've gotten a certain amount of money and then they stop because they value leisure more than they value just making endless amounts of money. That's governed by a kind of social norm where the Catholic Church says you need only as much money as sufficient to lead a good life, and beyond that there's no need to accumulate more money. And so there are a lot of examples where ideas are quite important in shaping what people want. I have realized that ideas are really important: you see them in all kind of different domains. Material conditions and ideas go together; it's a combination.

There are several historical ideas and events discussed in *The Origins of Political Order*, including transcendental religion, early individualism, family patterns and inheritance, church and state, the rule of law, the Renaissance, Luther, the creation of modern states, printing, and merito-cratic bureaucracies. What are the milestones in intellectual, political, and economic history that, according to you, were the main historical founda-tions of liberal democracies?

Yes, those are all important. But what is not commonly understood are these things about the family. I play this little game with my students sometimes. I ask them at what historical moment they think Europe-ans stopped living in extended families and began living in nuclear families. Most of them will give an answer that's way too late. They'll say the Industrial Revolution or the Renaissance or something like that, and the fact of the matter is that these extended kin groups had disappeared from Europe by the early Middle Ages. That is a history relatively few people recognize, but it was extremely important in or-der for liberalism to emerge. You can't really have a liberal society in a heavily kin-based social system. For instance, in India it is really hard to have a real liberal society because of the social pressures of families. Their families still make all these decisions, and when they get mar-ried, it's not a marriage of two individuals but of two families.

Probably not for kings and queens, but for the rest of the people, individu-alism came early?

Yes, and Marx got that wrong too, because he thought that it was the rise of the bourgeoisie that undermined the family, but I don't think the bourgeoisie would have risen if the family had not already been "ready."

The individual becomes important as well as those smaller families and the possibility to choose?

Yes. Individualism in the family is the mother of all individualisms. Inheritance was also important. Although their rights were not equal, it was much easier in Europe for women to inherit property than it was in China, India, the Middle East, or other strictly patrilineal societies. They always make sure that all of the resources go through the male side of the line, but in Europe that was different. These social foun-dations of individualism then get translated into an overt doctrine of liberalism. Many people don't understand how important the prior social evolution was.

Historical Sequencing Explains Today's Political Order

Fukuyama writes about sequencing, arguing that it matters enormously, both in *The Origins of Political Order* and in an article titled "Is There a Proper Sequence in Democratic Transitions?"

Is it the case that those countries in which "democracy preceded modern state building have had much greater problems achieving high-quality governance than those that inherited modern states from absolute monarchs," or is it the other way around?[2] And why do you also say that this sequencing might not apply today?

As a historical matter sequencing was pretty important. If you get a strong state as the first institution you create, a lot of times that prevents the emergence of either the rule of law or democracy. The state becomes so embedded and so strong that it prevents society from organizing. That was the situation in China; the European experience is quite different. You have law as the first institution and then a strong state that tries to emerge against the background of preexisting law. And so there's a big conflict between interests that want to pull the state back and the state that wants to expand its authority. In Europe you had a range of outcomes, from Russia, where the state "won," to Britain, where the law "won." Basically, the king was put under the law very early.

Creating democracy is the last step in the sequence. The general problem I have with sequencing policies is that you can't do sequencing deliberately. It just happened that this was a sequence in these different societies, but there's nobody in a position to say, "Okay, first we're going to do the rule of law and then fifty years later we're going to have a state, and then later we're going to have democracy." I mean, you can't just go to Denmark in that way. Nobody is in a position to make those kinds of decisions. Right now everybody wants everything simultaneously. And that's a problem because a lot of times the early introduction of democracy makes it very hard to consolidate a modern state. And the reason is that democracy creates demands for patronage.

The historical differences between countries have an impact on how these liberal democracies function today. The American bureaucracy has always been weaker, and belief in the state and social trust are lower than in Europe. How would you describe this matter today?

American distrust of the state is a little bit pathological, and it locks us into an equilibrium that we can't get out of. You don't trust the state, and therefore you don't want to pay taxes. You don't want to give the state authority, and therefore the state can't deliver public health care. Then when the state doesn't actually deliver goods and services, people say, "Well, see, the state is incompetent; I won't pay taxes or give it more authority." It's a vicious circle that a lot of countries in Latin America have followed as well as the United States.

Huntington's sequencing theory met strong criticism because he also argued that it would be better, if necessary, to go through an "authoritarian" phase before introducing democracy. He was accused of being authoritarian. Do you have any comments on the controversies around Huntington's claim that political order must be established before democracy, which was taken to be an acceptance of an authoritarian phase to establish order?

The authoritarian transition was a strategy that worked in East Asia but is not a universally valid one. You have a lot of countries that established both a state and something like democracy simultaneously, or at least made the transition to a modern state. It's just not the case that everybody has to go through this authoritarian stage.

Do you think that Huntington meant this?

I'm not sure he thought that was an absolutely necessary pattern, but he's the inventor of this authoritarian transition idea, which is prevalent in the East Asian model of having rapid economic growth occur under an authoritarian regime. It was a model that could be transferred to other countries. But it isn't very realistic that this model would have worked in Latin America in the 1970s, when you had all these military regimes around. Basically, you would be asking people to stay under these very nasty authoritarian regimes that, in any event, weren't doing very much for development.

Successfully Copying Practices

Your works cover much more than Europe and the United States. They include Southeast Asia, Japan, China, and selected countries in Africa and Latin America. What is your vision of development?

It's important not to fall into a kind of cultural determinism about certain parts of the world and say that they are never going to develop. If you go back one hundred years or so, it was a common opinion in the West that East Asia would never develop. You can get all these quotes about how China would never modernize because the Chinese weren't rational and didn't have this and that cultural practice. But here we are. In fact, there's one quote from Weber in his book on Confucianism and Taoism where he says something to the effect of "if there's any country less likely to modernize than China, it's Japan." So, you have to be a little bit careful about making these broad assertions.

In a book that you edited called *Falling Behind: Explaining the Development Gap between Latin America and the United States* from 2010, you and your coauthors discuss different reasons for the lack of a well-functioning political order in Latin America. How do these reasons fit into the picture about sequencing?

Latin America's "original sin" was the high degree of inequality it inherited from Spanish colonialism. Habsburg Spain created an extractive economic system to exploit the wealth of the Americas. In many parts of Latin America, class divisions were sharpened by ethnic divisions between Creoles and indigenous peoples. This has led to sharp polarizations in modern times as well as making economic development extremely difficult because growth is not broadly shared.

You have mentioned that Jared Diamond and Jeffrey Sachs have argued that material resources determine growth, but that others, like Daron Acemoglu and James Robinson, have rejected this argument.[3] On their view, resources count only when they are mediated through institutions. In a way, this reminds me of Norway. We found oil, but I believe it was the way we organized it that was the key to the Norwegian success. This stands in contrast to what happened with oil in Venezuela.

Well, again, you can find a lot of examples of where both ideas and social structure really affect outcomes over a long period of time. Let me back up a little bit and use Argentina as an example. There is this revival of thinking about the importance of climate and geography for outcomes. You can make a serious argument that what they call plantation agriculture was very bad for democracy. It is Jared Diamond's kind of thinking. You also have economic historians like Stanley Engerman and Kenneth Sokoloff who wrote this very famous article about Latin America and North America.[4] They argue that big plantation farms, like sugarcane or cotton, can use slave labor very easily, whereas wheat and corn are much more easily grown on family farms. And that was one of the explanations for why you have these very hierarchical societies in a lot of tropical countries and why family farming then led to greater democracy in North America.

If you look at the history of cotton in the United States, slavery was about to disappear at the time of the American Revolution, and then Eli Whitney invents the cotton gin. All of a sudden there are opportunities afforded by a big cash crop that's easily grown with slave labor. They import slaves and a lot of slave institutions from the Caribbean into the south of the United States, and that obviously had these very bad impacts on American society. So I think climate and geography are important.

However, if you think about the contrast between Argentina and North America, I think it shows the opposite—namely, that climate and geography aren't the only things that are important. Argentina should have developed like the American Midwest because it has a temperate climate; it's got a lot of open land for growing crops and cattle and an immigrant population from Europe. But at the very time in the 1860s when the US Congress was passing the Homestead Act that basically was taking all of this open land in the west and distributing it to family farmers, Argentina was concentrating land in the hands of a small number of wealthy families. That decision then had huge consequences a hundred years later because you have this landowning elite in Argentina that then became the backers of the military. So sometimes it could just be a case of a bad decision being taken. That's something you have to ask. There was a kind of democratic ideology in the United States that lay behind something like the Homestead Act, whereas in Argentina they still had these Span-ish authoritarian centralized systems.

More generally, how can other "lagging behind countries" reach a viable political order, and how do they get there, knowing that they do not have the centuries that Western European countries had?

The one advantage that any contemporary developing country has is that they don't have to reinvent the wheel. They do have practices from other countries that they can import, and although you cannot just import Denmark into any given country, at least it helps knowing that certain institutions have worked in other places. You can copy things, you can experiment, and if you're flexible and you don't try to rigidly copy everything, then I think you can make that work. Japan was one of the most successful countries when it comes to copying Western institutions. They said, "Well, these will work but these oth-ers won't," and they copied selectively based on what they thought their society could tolerate. Other countries, like Iran under the shah, weren't so successful. It was a rapid modernization model that created a big backlash in a conservative society. It's important that countries develop from their historical cultural past and that they are adapting their political systems to their own society.

How should we approach state building in emerging democracies?

It's very hard to find a lot of successful examples where foreign powers actually created durable state institutions that didn't collapse once the foreign power withdrew. Japan was not created by the Americans; it was a coherent modern society before the war. Americans didn't make it that way and, therefore, with respect to all the agencies that have been trying to do this work, there's a fairly spotty record. I wrote an article together with a friend of mine that's now going to go into the *Oxford Handbook of Governance*, and our conclusion is that it's very hard to point to a lot of data showing that there's been a lot of success in any kind of aggregate, measurable improvement in corruption in most parts of the developed and developing world. We argue that the reason for that is because it's in the elites' self-interest to be corrupt. Unless you can get them out of power and replace them with institutions that prevent that sort of behavior from occurring, you're not going to get very far. Therefore, most foreign actors do not have the leverage to actually bring about that kind of political transformation. That's the basic argument.

These elites need education. How can this be done?

We know that a good education system is important. We don't know if it will create an economic success, but it's a precondition. We do know that inclusive institutions are quite important. We don't know if it's enough. There is also a difference between the role of primary education and higher education. Much of the education efforts are very well-intentioned. Everything should be inclusive, and everybody should have access to education.

Take, for example, Papua New Guinea, where I did work back in the mid-2000s. It was very interesting because the first-generation leaders in Papua New Guinea had been trained at high schools built by the British. The problem there is incredible tribal fragmentation, with nine hundred different languages spoken in a country of 5 million people. The colonial authorities deliberately took high school students from different parts of the country and brought them to some place that wasn't their home territory, and every single one of the political leaders in the first generation after independence went to this one high school. They all knew each other, and it went pretty well. Then after that it fell apart, and the elites began sending their kids to private schools in Australia or New Zealand. They lost whatever shared experiences they had been given. There weren't elites that were able to communicate across these tribal boundaries any longer. For a long time, I thought that maybe we need to go back to focusing on higher education for some, and then you can expand that educational system to include everybody, but you got to focus on a narrow group of people first.

* * *

Samuel Huntington and Fukuyama might be closer to each other when it comes to the questions of sequencing, but Huntington was criticized for his argument that American identity was formed not only by formal political institutions but by the Anglo-Protestantism of the people who immigrated.

Notes

1. Fukuyama, *Political Order and Political Decay*, 7.

2. Fukuyama, 30.

3. Diamond, *Guns, Germs and Steel*; Sachs, *End of Poverty*; and Acemoglu and Robinson, *Why Nations Fail*.

4. Engerman et al., "Factor Endowments, Inequality, and Paths of Development."

ELEVEN

How Can We Understand How Societies Work?

So far we have talked about ideas and history. We now turn to how Fukuyama approaches his scholarly fields of interest. A persistent theme is Fukuyama's criticism of the methods and approach of the economist. A little background helps to explain Fukuyama's skepticism. He was recruited by Seymour Martin Lipset to George Mason University, where he was employed as professor of public policy from 1996 to 2001. In an article in memory of Lipset, Fukuyama wrote, "I spent five terrific years as his colleague at George Mason, where we initially occupied nearby offices in the double-wide trailer that was the first home of the Institute of Public Policy. Marty and I taught Public Policy 800, Culture and Public Policy, together every year, which was one of the most educational experiences I myself have ever had."[1] The course was about comparative analysis of different political systems, something that had been of interest to Lipset a long time.[2]

Yascha Mounk, in "The End of History Revisited," discusses Fukuyama's method and shows how the tradition of Lipset's empirical approach disappeared and was replaced by "quantitative political science, with focus on high-N statistical studies and rational-choice models."[3] This is far from what occupies Fukuyama and how he understands political development.

Comparative Analysis Is a Useful Approach

Let us turn to Seymour Martin Lipset, whom you met in the 1990s.

Yes, as I probably mentioned before, I left RAND and went to George Mason University, which was growing very rapidly. There was a chair that became vacant, and Marty recommended that they appoint me to it. So that was my first academic position. Most of what I feel I learned from Lipset had to do with American exceptionalism, because he had been writing about this from the beginning of his career. The last book he wrote was called *American Exceptionalism*.[4]

Even though the dedication is to Huntington, is Lipset "the godfather" of *The Origins of Political Order* **and** *Political Order and Political Decay*? **What can you tell me about how he influenced you and what you learned from each other?**

He really influenced my understanding of the United States and why it has such a different set of political institutions. Americans sometimes don't perceive how strange their own institutions are when you compare them to European ones or institutions in the democracies in Asia. I think Lipset helped me to understand that. Americans just have this deep abiding distrust of the state, and, for that reason, they've never been able to create a modern state in the way that other democracies have. They just had a different historical experience.

I am an economist and an intellectual historian. As I see it, you draw on history but also philosophy, sociology, psychology, and other relevant fields. You say somewhere that your aim was to present "a middle range theory that avoids the pitfalls both of excessive abstraction (the vice of economists) and excessive particularism (the problem of many historians and anthropologists)" and that you are "hoping to recover something of the lost tradition of nineteenth century historical sociology or comparative anthropology."[5] How would you describe the structure of your books about political order? How do you choose what to focus on?

Like I said in those quoted passages, you need a theoretical framework in order to look at the massive facts of history. But you can't start with the framework. You can't start by saying, "Well, I believe that the framework is X," then learn about all these different countries, and then try to cram them into the frame. This is the big problem with the Marxist tradition. Marx said that feudalism preceded capitalism. And so every Marxist scholar has to find feudalism in India and China and in places where it makes no sense at all. You don't want to do that, and you have to allow the theory to flow out of your knowledge of the empirical facts of these different countries' experiences.

You have to go back and forth?

Yes, sometimes the facts suggest that this theory is correct, and other times the theory is wrong. It's kind of a process. You have to just keep going back and forth. Sometimes you have to adjust the theory, and sometimes you learn facts that make you change everything. It's not a strict methodology.

You have obviously chosen to do comparative research on political order. You choose all kinds of different countries all over the globe to explain different systems, and the books on political order are huge volumes presenting a lot of information.

Yes, it's sort of an intellectual arrogance. But I think it's actually useful. Many scholars draw generalizations based on one or even two regions. But then it turns out that there's yet another region that completely contradicts these generalizations, or else supports them, or you find that there are commonalities across regions that you didn't really think had anything to do with one another. So, for example, I wrote in my chapters on China about this famous hypothesis about why the modern state arose in early modern Europe, which had to do with warfare.[6] As far as I can see, that theory applies perfectly well to ancient China. The Chinese have this strong state tradition in that they fought wars for five hundred years that had all the same effects that wars did in Europe. But, as far as I'm aware, nobody else has ever pointed this out, because people were not used to comparing across regions and historical periods.

I saw that you dedicated your state-building book to Lipset. How did his thought contribute to that work?

His influence probably had to do with the fact that the state-building book was about this practical effort to create a state.

You mention several times that Lipset used to say, "A person who knows only one country knows no countries." And you wrote when he died, "It is

only by looking across different societies that one can understand what is either typical or unique about one's own."[7] You also mention the small-*N* comparative approach. Can you explain what the small-*N* comparative approach is to readers who are not familiar with political science?

There are basically three different approaches to understanding social behavior. One is a large-*N* approach, which is the dominant statistical approach, where you have as large a sample size as possible and then use different statistical techniques to try to establish causality. Then you have at the opposite end, what historians and anthropologists do, which is a single *N* where you basically just study one society and study it in an extremely great detail. In between, you've got the small-*N* approach—which is really not very much used anymore—in which you do comparison. We try to combine some of the richness of the single-*N* studies and the scale of the large-*N* ones. You also do a comparative analysis so that you can try to draw some generalizations. You can recognize patterns of political order. I suppose at this point you would have to say that there is a fourth approach, which is to do experiments in which you compare one community that has undergone some kind of change or intervention with a control community that is evenly matched but did not receive the intervention.

It's a good thing that you revived the small-*N* tradition.

Well, I don't know. I don't think I've revived it. You have to compare, but with a sophisticated understanding of the particular contexts of the countries you are comparing.

Culture and Institutions Are Important

In *Falling Behind*, Fukuyama says that many people think institutions are "formal, visible, macropolitical rules defined by constitutions and law—presidencies, electoral systems, federalism, and the like."[8] Formal institutions can relatively easily be altered, but not the informal ones. Further, Fukuyama quotes Huntington in an article about political dysfunction: "Institutions are 'stable, valued, recurring patterns of behavior,' as Huntington put it, the most important function of which is to facilitate collective action."[9]

These are all issues that are important for understanding how societies function. Culture and norms are "sticky" and usually change slowly. We are loyal to institutions maybe even long after they are deteriorating, because they decay slowly, and it might be difficult to discover that they are doing so.

We must talk about institutions. They are increasingly important to understand, and well-functioning institutions are paramount to liberal democracy. Do you share Huntington's view and definition?

Huntington's is a much more specific definition of institutions than the one used by Douglass North. North simply said that an institution was a rule, while Huntington said institutions were stable, valued, recurring, and autonomous, which provides a lot more texture. Institutions are critical because they serve a coordinating function. That's why you have an institution. You can't have human cooperation if you don't have rules. Institutions were just persistent rules that make it possible for people to work together. North and other institutional economists emphasize property rights as the most important institution providing for economic growth. Property rights are important, but because of North they were overemphasized in the development world.[10] There are many other institutions that made possible the modern world. The idea that you need to think about institutions when explaining economic growth is not something that I, or anyone else, would dispute at this point.

It is important that institutions have an integrating effect over time, that they are coherent with their societies, and that they include all members. In societies where these practices are prominent, there will be tools for handling conflict and disagreements. Can you give some examples of such inclusive institutions?

It could be different from country to country or from society to society. Obviously, franchise is the most basic one, and it's interesting how late the franchise was universalized in Western countries. Women didn't even get the right to vote in some Swiss cantons until the 1960s. It's late, but many countries we regard as good democracies didn't give women the right to vote until the early nineteenth century. When did it happen in Norway?

It was early, in 1913.

Yes, you know, that's been the primary mechanism of inclusion. I have now focused on other kinds of topics. So, for example, the issue for women is no longer juridical equality. That's been established a long time ago. The question is more social equality and behavior in workplaces, with women working. So, the #MeToo movement is really almost entirely about social norms and how men are expected to behave. It is the same thing with the acceptance of gays, lesbians, and transgender people. That's something that came later, and there was a juridical part to it. That is not something that you can legislate only; it has to be internalized.

In 2004 you asked some questions about institutions yourself. The field of research was, in your words, chaotic. Many things had been added to the pot, making it difficult to discern which of the concepts in the stew were important. In your book *The Great Disruption*, you write about norms, culture, and social capital. Conservatism may hinder changes in institutions and might therefore be a source of decay. I remember that you have used the example of the US Forest Service.

The problem in the US Forest Service was the same as in many other institutions. It was too rigid. The Forest Service got captured by special interests, and then it stopped functioning in the way that people expected. In the case of the Forest Service, a lot of the problems had to do with the fact that it had multiple missions. The firefighting mission became central to it, which was not the original mission. The original mission was to provide sustainable forestry. But because people started wanting to have houses built in woodland areas where they really shouldn't build in the first place, the Forest Service had to protect them. And when technical experts said, "Actually, this can't really protect people in a cost-effective way," the homeowners used their political influence to get Congress to tell the Forest Service, "No, you still have to protect them." Anyhow, that's why we're in this situation we're in right now, where the Forest Service spends tens of billions of dollars a year fighting fires. I mean, these things can happen in many different types of institutions. The US Forest Service is just one example.

How important are these unwritten rules, norms, and practices that make institutions work? And are they more important than the written rules and organizational structures?

There's a built-in conservatism to human institutions. People don't like to change readily, and there are probably good evolutionary reasons why that's the case. Human beings value stability and predictability. Often if you want to get really big adaptations, it requires something like a war or a revolution or a huge economic crisis before people begin to see that their institutions aren't functioning very well. I had hopes, you know, after the financial crisis in 2008, that this would be a wake-up call that American institutions weren't working properly. But in the end, I think it wasn't a severe enough crisis compared to, let's say, the Great Depression when unemployment had gone up to 25 percent. That laid the foundations for the modern American welfare state. Even the current COVID-19 crisis is proving not to be severe enough to bring about larger reforms; rather than ending polarization, the American response to the crisis has been undermined by our polarized response to it.

Can you give a short overview of the framework you used in *Falling Behind* to describe how formal constitutional setups have pros and cons and how they interact with informal political culture?

The problem in Latin America, where most countries gained independence from Spain or Portugal in the nineteenth century, was that they adopted constitutions that were in many cases replicas of the American Constitution, but they didn't have the underlying norms and cultural values to support that kind of constitution. Most Latin American societies were based on Spanish and Portuguese colonial practices. First of all, they were very unequal because they were settler societies in which you had a relatively small European population sitting on top of a very large indigenous population. But the institutions most Spaniards and Portuguese brought with them were also very authoritarian. You had a class conflict in which elites wanted to protect their privileges. Then there was an attempt to introduce democracy, but leaders used those democratic rules to protect themselves through clientelism and political patronage. That's really what's happened in several places in South America.

Understanding Institutions

We have already touched upon this when we talked about the Chicago school, but it is interesting to discuss the whole picture of this reductionist understanding of human beings and also of institutions. As I understand it, new institutional economics is more concerned with other aspects of society than institutional structures.

New institutional economics was used to describe what Douglass North had done in economics and in social sciences, at least in the United States.[11] He defines institutions simply as a persistent rule. Institutions can be formal, like a law, or can be informal, like a cultural norm. To me it's kind of unbelievable that, prior to him, economists didn't pay any attention to institutions. Political scientists understood that they were important right from the beginning, whereas economists had a neoclassical model based on rational utility maximization that didn't have institutions in it. Then economists began to realize that wasn't sufficient, and they started to learn what political scientists had understood, except that it was more than a generation later.

How would you comment on the economists' understanding of institutions?

A lot of this is an academic dispute. If you look at the economists that have been writing about development broadly—Douglass North, my colleague Barry Weingast, and people like Daron Acemoglu and James Robinson—in my view, they've revived this very crude version of modernization theory. Here at Stanford, there are a number of protégés of Douglass North. He is the economist who really brought history back into economics, but he remains an economist at heart, because for much of his career he focused only on the material conditions driving human behavior. North and his students have this whole historical narrative about how modern property rights came about as a result of the Glorious Revolution in seventeenth-century England, and that explains all subsequent economic growth.[12] Acemoglu and Robinson mostly talk about "inclusive institutions," which start with property rights and add in liberal rule of law plus some kind of democratic accountability, but then they throw a strong state into this mix as well.[13] It's a kind of kitchen sink approach, and they've been criticized for having such a broad definition of institutions that their theory becomes tautological: if you have good institutions, you'll have good institutions.

In the social sciences, these macro theories have moved us backward fifty years to when you had this very crude version of modernization theory. In fact, there are many institutions. This was an important topic in my recent conversation with Deirdre McCloskey.[14] She has argued that property rights are one of several critical institutions, but it's not clear that they're the most important. You have countries like China that have developed extremely rapidly. They've got institutions, but they're not respecting anything like Western property rights.

In reality, it is much more complicated. It's not that easy. Deirdre is really contemptuous of this whole theory. She says it was the change that came with the Scientific Revolution that was really critical. You just needed this openness and curiosity to new ideas, willingness to take intellectual risks. That's what was critical. I've always believed some version of that. You can't really explain how modernization happened if you don't follow the development of European thought in that period.

Can you go back a bit further and talk about how the nineteenth-century notion of political economy was reduced to economics?

I think it's basically correct that throughout the nineteenth century there was no separate field of economics, and everybody wrote in this political economy tradition. You did have these schools, like the German Historical school in the nineteenth century that basically took a historical sociological view of the development of institutions.[15] But then this changed, especially in the Anglo-Saxon intellectual world after Léon Walras and Alfred Marshall.[16] They introduced the ideas of marginalism and equilibrium and laid the basis for a much more rigorous but at the same time reduced understanding of economics that founded on certain microeconomic concepts. All of a sudden modern classical economics was born based on a much-reduced set of assumptions and principles. Economists no longer thought of themselves as political economists, because they thought they could explain economic behavior based on this kind of simplified rationality that took into account only economic factors.

If we go back even further to Adam Smith and to David Hume, who talked about custom and habits, was this understanding of economy and society also lost?

I think that's why the social sciences went backward: Economists and many social scientists forgot about all of these things.

* * *

This critique of economists also got the attention of Branko Milanović. In his blog post "Francis Fukuyama against Mainstream Economics," he writes, "I noticed among my notes a number of Fukuyama's views on economics, many directly critical of some mainstream nostrums. Because I think that few economists have read Fukuyama, and perhaps even fewer have read him attentively, and perhaps even fewer have read the entire book, I decided to bring up Fukuyama's several economic statements." The lack of understanding among economists of how history and institutions affect economic growth hits a nerve. Milanović has changed his view on Fukuyama after reading his two books on political order, and he believes that economists deserve Fukuyama's criticism. Fukuyama, as we have seen, does not like the economic reductionist approach and analyses.

Notes

1. Fukuyama, "Seymour Martin Lipset 1922–2006."
2. Lipset, *American Exceptionalism*.
3. Mounk, "End of History Revisited," 26.
4. Lipset (1922–2006) was a well-known American sociologist who published several works about the conditions for democracy in comparative perspective. *American Exceptionalism* was published in 1995.
5. Fukuyama, *Origins of Political Order*, 24.
6. Fukuyama, *Origins of Political Order*, chapters 6, 7, and 8.
7. Fukuyama, "Seymour Martin Lipset 1922–2006."
8. Fukuyama, *Falling Behind*, 195.
9. Fukuyama, "America in Decay."
10. North, Wallis, and Weingast, *Violence and Social Orders*.
11. North, *Institutions, Institutional Change and Economic Performance*.
12. North and Weingast, "Constitutions and Commitment."
13. Acemoglu and Robinson, *Why Nations Fail*.
14. McCloskey, *How to Be Human—Though an Economist*.

15. The German Historical school argued that history and empirical knowledge was the basis for knowledge about human actions and economic matters. Economics was culture-specific, not general.

16. Marshall (1842–1924) was the founder of neoclassical economics, and his most famous book was *Principles of Economics* from 1890.

TWELVE

Is Identity Politics a Question of *Thymos?*

Fukuyama has been thinking and writing about identity for many years, and, as we have seen, the emergence of identity politics is one of the trends that has changed world politics after 1989. Identity was a substantial part of *The End of History*, where one of the main hypotheses is that history is moving toward modernization and liberal democracy because of the universal human desire for recognition— what Fukuyama calls *thymos. Thymos* is a word used by Plato in *The Republic* to refer to a part of the soul that seeks recognition of one's value or dignity. This idea reappears as Hegel's desire for recognition, a desire for self-esteem that we all seek from others. This universal desire for recognition is the main reason why liberal democracy is the most complete political system since it allows universal recognition. Fukuyama argues that liberal democracy is the only political system that can make complete recognition possible.

Fukuyama believes that all political systems, including liberal democracies, need to have a sense of national identity. In a democracy, that identity has to be inclusive and based on democratic principles, an identity in which citizens can take pride. Recognition comes about through the granting of rights; for a democracy to work, citizens must recognize each other's rights and have their own rights respected. It must be a defining value of democracy; it must be internalized.

Thymos as a Foundational Value Driving Human Motivation

Turning to your new—and I would also say old—idea of the foundational value of recognition. I can see this idea in almost all of your books, including *Our Posthuman Future*, and to me it is key to understanding current political developments. You first treat recognition extensively in *The End of History and the Last Man*, but many readers, it seems to me, have become aware of your interest in recognition with the publication of *Identity* in September 2018.

Identity is the belief that one has an inner self and that that self is not being adequately respected or recognized by other people. It can take lots of forms. It can take an individual form, as when one believes that one's true self is not being recognized. Or it can take a group form in terms of one's membership in a group that one thinks is not being respected adequately. If you don't get that respect, it leads to a lot of anger. Identity is much more connected to the emotions than it is to reason. One of the oldest forms of identity was nationalism, where particular cultural groups demanded recognition in the form of having their own state that corresponds to the boundaries of the cultural group. But it can take other forms as well: especially groups that are marginalized by race, by ethnicity, by gender, by sexual orientation, and so forth.

Tell me the story from the beginning—when did you hear about *thymos* first? What caught your interest?

It started with my study of Plato's *Republic* with Allan Bloom. This is a big theme in book four of *The Republic*, so it goes all the way back to my first year at the university. This is when it started, and Bloom was also the role model for Saul Bellow's novel *Ravelstein*. He was really a remarkable teacher. In *The Republic*, Socrates is talking about human nature. And he says, "Well, we know that there's logos for reason, and we know that there's desire," but he says, "Isn't there a third part of the soul that is the seat of anger?" I referred to the Greek word *thymos*, which Plato uses in book four of *The Republic*, which means anger in modern Greek. We feel anger when our inner worth is not recognized, and we demand respect. This is a very powerful emotion, and it is not what we would today call our economic self-interest or our rational economic self-interest. We want other people to esteem us as we think we deserve, connected to the emotions of pride and shame. This is important because it's something different from the economists' understanding of human behavior. It's very important to see that a lot of human motivation is driven by this desire for recognition.

You write for the first time in *The End of History* about isothymia and of megalothymia. A particularly interesting passage from that book reads,

> The passion for equal recognition . . . does not necessarily diminish with the achievement of greater de facto equality and material abundance but may actually be stimulated by it. Tocqueville explained that when the differences between social classes or groups are great and supported by long-standing tradition, people become resigned or accepting of them. But when society is mobile and groups pull closer to one another, people become more acutely aware and resentful of the remaining differences.[1]

What are isothymia and megalothymia, and can you also explain the inherent contradiction between the two?

Isothymia has to do with a desire to be recognized as the equal of other people. Megalothymia is the desire to be recognized as superior. Obviously, democratic societies have to be based in some way on the control of megalothymia. But oftentimes they are linked to one another. A lot of times you start out desiring equal recognition, isothymia, but then you switch over into demanding superior recognition. This is the story of most nationalisms. I think you want to be recognized. The Germans wanted initially just to be another country in Europe with a single German government and, once they got that, they started to want to dominate. *Isothymia* and *megalothymia* pertain to both nations or groups and to individuals.

Can you explain how the idea traveled from Plato to Hegel and onward?

Well, I don't know if there is a direct connection. Hegel did not quote Plato in this regard, but he did talk about the struggle for recognition as the driver of the whole historical process, and he put it in very abstract terms. It's between masters and slaves. There's a dialectic of the master and the slave. The master wants to be recognized by the slave but then begins to realize over time that the recognition of a slave is not worth very much. The slave is not a full human being, because the slave is not willing to risk his life in a bloody battle. The only way of solving this problem is by shifting to universal recognition, where everybody recognizes the essential humanity of everybody else. Then you're recognized by somebody that's worthy of recognizing you in a certain sense.

You describe the path to modern identity, starting with *thymos*. Then, you discuss Martin Luther and Jean-Jacques Rousseau and the inner self. Finally, you arrive at dignity for all and the modern self. This modern dignity and recognition you have called a fork: universal recognition of individual rights and collective recognition based on the nation. Can you explain this framework and the fork?

It starts with the French Revolution, out of which emerge two political movements. The first is a liberal regime based on universal recognition. The Rights of Man that you are granted in a liberal society are a recognition of your individual dignity as a citizen. You're given a right to speak, to associate, to believe, and finally to vote. This means you're given a share of political power, which means that you are recognized as being capable of self-government. In an authoritarian regime, on the other hand, you are regarded, at best, as a child that needs to be guided by the state or else simply as something to be used by the state for its own purposes.

But the other political movement that emerged from the French Revolution was nationalism, which was a particularistic form of recognition. Nationalism is based on group identity, a group that shares a common language and culture. Liberalism and nationalism are the two forces that then contend with each other throughout Europe for the next century. Ultimately, I think the nationalistic form of recognition dominates and leads to a disaster for European civilization in the world wars.

Yes, for many European countries, nationalism has an unpleasant ring.

The first great manifestation of identity politics was European nationalism in the nineteenth century. The classic case was Germany. There were Germans scattered all over Central and Eastern Europe who didn't have their own state. A united German state was said to be necessary for Germans to receive the dignity that they deserved. We need our own state to govern ourselves instead of being split across all over Europe. That was the driver that led to German unification, to Italian unification, and ultimately to the formation of these nation-states that then went on to agendas that were aggressive, intolerant, and ultimately that led to the two world wars in the first half of the twentieth century.

Criticism of *Thymos* from Left and Right

When *thymos* **was introduced in** *The End of History and the Last Man*, **it was not disputed. Have the reactions and criticism been more prevalent now, or did you get them back in the 1990s as well?**

Yes, I have written about identity all these years. My experience in the 1990s was that nobody read that part of the book, so it just disappeared. There was a small number of people who understood the argument and appreciated it. Interestingly, it is included in a book by Peter Sloterdijk, a German philosopher who has a whole chapter on my treatment of *thymos*.[2]

Your idea about the three parts of the soul and the way you use it to explain group thinking and the basis of identity politics has also met criticism. How do you argue to counter these objections?

I didn't receive any substantial criticism in the 1990s. But today it is met mainly with curiosity. One of Sloterdijk's students used my conception of *thymos*, mostly as a positive political value, in his work. This student is now a member of the AfD, the right-wing populist Alternative for Germany party. I was in Germany, and I got some questions about this: "Isn't this kind of a right-wing idea?" I actually don't think it is a right-wing ideology, because it's just meant to be a psychological category.

So that's how you counter the objections. You tell your critics what the idea of *thymos* **actually is?**

Yes, the book is really stimulated by an effort to understand the sources of the populist votes in many democratic countries. My view is that it begins with economic inequality. But that's not sufficient to explain the particular character of this revolt, because anger over inequality should have empowered left-wing parties. But instead you have these right-wing populist groups that have taken power in Italy, in the United States, in Hungary, and in other places. I think the reason for that is, what's driving a lot of those voters is less a concern over resources and economics per se than about identity.

In terms of the criticism I've gotten, I think that a lot of it comes from my attempt to give a historical account of where identity comes from. I argue that it started on the Left and then has gravitated over to the Right. A lot of people somehow got the idea that my main critique was of left-wing identity movements, but the concern was always with right-wing ones because I think they're actually a threat to democracy itself. I don't think the left-wing parties particularly threaten democracy. In fact, their key demand is simply for democracy to fulfill its promise in terms of equality.

What about #MeToo and Black Lives Matter? What is it concretely that these movements want? Is there ever a level where they will find that recognition is fulfilled?

Probably not, because if you think about something like the #MeToo movement, it is not only partly a matter of policy or legislation, such as broadening definitions of rape or sexual assault. It involves more of a cultural change, in which men come to recognize that the traditional sexualized ways in which they treat women are actually acts of disrespect. That kind of change is happening gradually and may never be fully fulfilled. You can get a broad social change, but it's never going to be completely fulfilled. It is the same thing with race. Some people may pay lip service to racial equality but continue to harbor prejudices and stereotypes and so forth. It's more about norms than legal changes. Today many of the groups that people are organizing around are based on fixed characteristics that are not voluntary. And this is different from joining a group where you have shared interests with others.

Some have criticized you for blaming the left wing.

It is just a complicated interaction because left identity politics produced what we call political correctness, where you don't want to say anything that diminishes the dignity of anyone, including groups that you've never heard of before. All of a sudden if you talk in a certain way that's demeaning to someone, it creates an indignant reaction, even though the same phrase uttered a few years or even months earlier wouldn't have drawn any comment. There's been a reaction against this kind of political correctness, where a lot of times politicians find they can't actually say anything because they're too afraid of offending some particular group. That's why Donald Trump can get away with being offensive to everybody because people say, "Well, I may not agree with him particularly, but at least he's honest."

I would like to draw attention to another value, tolerance—which is to allow something unpleasant and unlikable. Why is it so important in liberal democracies to recognize, not only tolerate?

The problem is that in many parts of society, you're trying to make formal rules to regulate tolerance where you can't really do that. The formal rule actually intrudes on other sorts of goods that society wants. The clearest case has to do with quotas. Everybody agrees there should be more women and minorities represented in management, but meritocracy is also an important value.

People want to be esteemed. That's part of human nature's idea of *thymos* as being a constitutive third part of the soul. People's satisfaction in life oftentimes is more related to the esteem with which they're held than the material resources that they have. They want to be respected for something, not only tolerated.

Is everything governed by the quest for dignity?

Well, let me just give you the contemporary example of the gay marriage movement. Was that driven by economic considerations or was it driven by this kind of dignity politics? I think that there were economic issues involved. Couples wanted rights of survivorship, of inheritance, but all of those legal provisions could have been provided in civil unions. But the advocates of gay marriage said we want our unions to be treated with dignity, to have the same status as a marriage between a man and a woman. It was really about recognition that persuaded people across an amazing number of countries to legalize that particular institution.

Identity Issues and the Political System

We have been concentrating on groups' and individuals' feelings and identity, but this does also have effects for political parties, for how we vote, and whom we vote for. Different voting systems may also have great consequences for how political parties develop.

We have a plethora of political parties in Norway and Scandinavia, whereas the United Kingdom and the United States have two blocks. You wrote about different parliamentary systems in *Falling Behind*. Tell me how you see party systems and how they evolve. How do you place the countries today that you discussed in *Falling Behind*?

Party systems will differ based on the social cleavages that exist in different countries. But let's take two-party systems like the ones that exist in the United States and Britain. This has been discussed by political scientists for decades, and I think it's fairly well understood. The reason that you get two-party systems is because of the electoral system. If you have a first-past-the-post or plurality voting system, you're likely to get two dominant parties according to something called Duverger's law.[3] If you vote for a third party, you're often going to empower the party that you liked the least. With proportional representation, on the other hand, a vote for a small party doesn't necessarily mean that your least-favorite party is going to do better. The problem with a proportional representation system is that sometimes it fragments power too much, and it's really hard to get a coalition that can act.

Is the election system the problem?

I don't think just the fact of elections is the problem. There are many other institutional features that make American democracy problematic. One is obviously campaign finance. Basically, anything goes in terms of corporations' and rich individuals' financing of elections. The other thing is our electoral system. It's a first-past-the-post system where it discourages third-party candidates. Finally, both parties having moved to popular primaries encourages extremism because the people that vote in primaries tend to be activists in both parties. That tends to privilege the more extreme wings of the party because they're the ones that get out to vote in these very low-turnout elections. All of those things could be changed. We could mitigate the polarization problem somewhat by moving to something called ranked-choice voting, a system that is used in Australia.

How does that work?

Instead of voting for one candidate, you vote for a ranked list, and you say who's your first choice, your second choice, and your third choice. And if your first choice is not among the top candidates, your vote is redistributed to your second choice. It encourages alliances between candidates because they want to get the second preferences of their rivals, but it also means that if you don't like the choice that has been put before you by the two parties, you can vote for a third party safely. That would do something to lessen the polarization that our two-party system produces today.

This is your preferred voting system?

It's one of those permanent tradeoffs, where there's no optimal system. A two-party system can be very functional if something needs to get done. If one party gets a majority, even if it's based on artificially augmenting the leading party's vote, then it can enable legislation. Whereas in a lot of coalition governments in Europe, you have an election, and the result is that you add a few more Christian Democrats, a few less Greens or something, but basically the government doesn't really change. People get frustrated with that. They can't actually get the kind of big change that they want. At the other extreme is the classic Westminster system, which consists of a parliamentary system combined with a first-past-the-post electoral system. Most political scientists have concluded that neither system is really optimal; the first disperses power and the second concentrates power excessively. Something like the German system, mixed-member proportionality, tries to reduce the number of parties and fragmentation by having a 5 percent threshold. It also retains overall proportionality. Also, single-member districts that represent particular constituencies are a good compromise.

A while ago you wrote the following: "In place of the Left–Right ideological split defined largely by issues revolving around the relative economic power of capital and labor in an industrialized setting that characterized 20th-century politics, we now have a political spectrum organized increasingly around identity issues, many of which are defined more by culture than by economics narrowly construed. This shift is not good for the health of liberal democracy."[4] Are we going from political parties to identity groups? Those huge political parties, like the Social Democrats and the Christian Democrats, do you think they're losing ground permanently?

Yeah. That's generally the shift that's being taking place. I think it is bad for democracy overall. The traditional Social Democrats began to lose touch with the old working class that had formerly been their biggest source of votes. This has happened across the board with a lot of left-wing parties. Social Democrats in many countries have gotten a lot weaker, and many of those voters have turned to voting for right-wing identity parties that represented a backlash against this liberal, open world that had shifted the cultural basis of their societies. So that's my explanation for why the Right has done relatively well in the new forms of populism that are the most dynamic.

Brexit voters and Trump voters can be divided to a certain extent by education level and also by age, which again probably says more about education than age itself. Thomas Piketty has, in a recent study, looked at educational patterns and votes, showing that left-wing parties now get votes from people with higher education.[5] He sees it as a return to class as an identity marker. You are say in "American Political Decay or Renewal? The Meaning of the 2016 Election" that "American democracy is finally responding to the rise of inequality and the economic stagnation experienced by most of the population. Social class is now back at the heart of American politics, trumping other cleavages—race, ethnicity, gender, sexual orientation, geography—that had dominated discussion in recent elections." Is education then an identity marker and a divider?

It is a divider but one that gets expressed culturally in a strange way. Today's upper class does not perceive itself to be a ruling class: most well-educated professionals today tend to be ideologically on the Left; they profess concern for excluded and marginalized people and vote for left-of-center parties. In cultural terms, they are more cosmopolitan and comfortable with all sorts of diversity. Nonetheless, by the choices they make regarding their children and their own lives, they tend to reinforce their advantages as a class.

Are we returning to class? What do you understand by class?

Yes, in a way, we are returning to class divisions as long as you understand that it gets expressed in the cultural terms I just outlined. Our new upper class is defined by education and meritocracy. They are not the old rentier class that simply inherited their money, and what they pass on to their children is not a trust fund but rather access to elite education that improves their children's life chances. Branko Milanović points out that this division is reinforced by associative mating, where well-educated people tend to marry each other and produce children with similar advantages. The upper class is also defined by residence; they tend to live in large urban agglomerations with good job opportunities for well-educated people. Whether COVID-19 will start changing this is an interesting question.

What about social mobility?

There are a number of studies that indicate that in the United States, at least, intergenerational social mobility has been dropping. This has been reinforced by the ability of educated parents to pass on their advantages through a variety of mechanisms, including their greater propensity to stay married and raise children in stable households. The opposite has been happening in working-class households, where increasing numbers of children are being raised in single-parent families.

At least in Europe, the existence of a variety of political parties contributes to well-functioning societies. How important are these parties, and do they still have a chance to contribute in the future? Or will we see others replacing them—and can they be expected to be as inclusive?

They're all critical to the system. The problem lies particularly with the established political parties. They've lost voters, and they've lost legitimacy in the eyes of a lot of people because they haven't responded adequately to the kinds of social pressures that those societies are facing now.

Let's take France. You have Emmanuel Macron and En Marche!, which was completely new in that political system. Do you think that France is an example of how things will go in other countries, or is this just France?

Macron is one leader who has tried to revive centrism, and En Marche! did win the vote. In a modern democracy, people don't just say, "Well, we voted in an election and that's that." But this did not solve France's problems, as we saw with the emergence of the *gilets jaunes* [yellow vest] movement. There are still a large number of French voters who are disaffected by the new politics and also by Macron's personal style.

You have previously drawn a parallel between Roosevelt and Mussolini. Why?

Roosevelt and Mussolini were both populists but with very different agendas and outcomes. Roosevelt used anger over the Depression to build an American welfare state, while Mussolini used his power to create a fascist dictatorship. The populist mobilization we are witnessing today can both create good things and also end in catastrophes. This is also a key point in David Runciman's book *How Democracy Ends*, which looks in depth at what history can teach us about authoritarian takeovers of liberal democracies. In the 1930s, the situation was similar when it came to economic problems and political discontent. In Europe this led to Adolf Hitler and Benito Mussolini, and in the United States to Franklin Roosevelt and the New Deal. It depends on how politicians and elites channel the discontent.

A recent article argued that voters have become ungovernable: "Compared to voters in the decades following World War II, voters of the twenty-first century have an increased sense of entitlement, a higher regard for themselves and their opinions, and a less tolerant view of others. They are more demanding, more vitriolic and more thin-skinned. And it is not just millennials and Generation X. These changes apply to the baby boomer generation as well."[6] How would you comment on this?

I mean, it may be happening. It's hard to know whether this is just a cyclical phenomenon that has to do with the rise of certain kinds of populist voters or whether this is permanent. It's entirely possible that this represents a shift in people's expectations of government and government responsiveness, so it can be, but I don't know.

In a parliamentary political system, laws will be prepared in ministries by a competent bureaucracy. The ministries, represented by the minister, will be responsible to the parliament and ultimately to the voters. This political organization will facilitate a long-term, strategic perspective. Courts in Europe have generally avoided encroaching on legislative prerogatives as they have in the United States, though that may be changing. The laws are more coherent, and they are to a lesser extent exposed to influence from powerful interest groups.

You also visited a number of European countries when you published *Identity*. Do you see the same challenges there?

Every country is different. Belgium has long-standing difficulties getting a government established. I was there recently, and they've got a big identity problem because of the big split between Flanders and Wallonia, and governance suffers as a result. They've got big problems in public administration because they're highly decentralized and because they can't agree on a strong central government. That's hurt them in terms of things like controlling terrorism because they have multiple intelligence agencies that don't share information with each other.

* * *

Germany, the Netherlands, and the Scandinavian countries have succeeded in maintaining a stronger trust in the state over time, based on greater underlying social consensus, making it easier to implement reforms. On the other side of the spectrum, we have Italy, which has low trust in the state and tension between regions. Italians don't necessarily see themselves as a single country. It is important to understand how identity influences politics and how voting systems and political parties are affected.

Notes

1. Fukuyama, *End of History and the Last Man*, 295.
2. Sloterdijk, *Rage and Time*.

3. A simple definition of Duverger's law holds that "the simple majority, single ballot system favours the two-party system." OxfordReference.com, https://www.oxfordreference.com/viewbydoi/10.1093/acref/9780199207800.013.0382.

4. Fukuyama, "Clash at 25."

5. Piketty, "Brahmin Left vs Merchant Right."

6. Stitt, "Rise of the Ungovernable."

THIRTEEN

How Do Society and Capitalism Interact?

Economic growth, innovations, and a capitalist system are usually connected with democracy, although the last few decades have shown that countries like China and Singapore have had rapid economic growth but not democracy. It is also true, as Branko Milanović states in his book *Capitalism Alone*, that the political or authoritarian capitalism in these countries, which also includes Vietnam and Burma, has to promise economic growth. And since political capitalism is not restricted by the rule of law, it is in its essence based on arbitrary decisions, which makes corruption prevalent. Western liberal meritocratic capitalism works under the rule of law.

Social Capital and Trust Are Important for Economic Growth

I've been studying how self-interest appeared in Europe, especially in French thought, before Adam Smith. For instance, the Jansenist Pierre Nicole was strictly religious, but he wrote about self-interest and how results mattered, and this perception established a way of looking at trade that made it acceptable, even for those immensely religious Jansenist monks. This, of course, was long before Weber. How do you see these ideas?

I am thinking of this very nice little book by Albert Hirschman, *The Passions and the Interests*.

Yes, Hirschman explains this well. It is the essence of "rhetoric" and the importance of ideas, what Deirdre McCloskey has called "the bourgeois virtues," that Hirschman framed as the passions and interests. McCloskey was trying to establish a story of how the virtues and capitalism interact. It was actually quite interesting reading through her books, especially because

the moral conditions that she argues are important for capitalism are also important to liberal democracy. Do you know her work?[1]

Actually, it's funny. I had never met Deirdre McCloskey until February 2019. We sat next to each other at a conference just by accident. It turns out we agree on so many things. After that, she recently turned up for one of my lectures in Italy.

McCloskey began by critiquing the materialist, rational-choice model underlying modern economic theory. As I mentioned earlier, she thought that Douglass North's theory of modernization was terribly oversimplified because it largely ignored the importance of ideas. North says that modern economic growth was made possible by the development of institutions like property rights in the seventeenth century but then fails to give an account of why this emerged at that point. Deirdre's work emphasizes the importance both of ideas and of virtues like the work ethic and belief in the dignity of ordinary labor. She is an heir to Albert O. Hirschman, whose book *The Passions and the Interests* provides an intellectual history of the transition from an aristocratic honor-based culture to a bourgeois one in this period.

The subtitle of your book *Trust* is *The Social Virtues and the Creation of Prosperity*. First, enlighten us on the main issues that you are discussing in this book. And second, explain what you mean by social capital and by trust.

I've already related the story of how my publisher, Erwin Glikes, asked me what I wanted to do for a second book after *The End of History*. I had always been interested in the question of culture and economics because it seemed to me that there were cultural patterns that showed up in economic behavior. I remember once reading about how, during World War II, some British commandos captured a German radar set in France and brought it back to England, where they took it apart. They couldn't believe how well the parts were machined, and they said, "We couldn't have produced this radar in Britain, because we just don't have the machinists available to produce something like this." That has always struck me as really interesting. Why should it be? Why should these two modern European countries be so different in their craft traditions? So, I said to my publisher, "I would like to write about this." I didn't have this idea of social capital and trust yet.

I just started reading and, just like in the case of *The End of History*, it was a big opportunity for self-education. I had maybe a year to write the book. I spent the first months just reading all of the things I had wanted to read for a long time and never had a chance to. I actually read through a lot of classical social theory, including Weber, Durkheim, Tönnies, Ernst Troeltsch, Sombart, and Thorstein Veblen. I was trying to come up with some particular angle by which culture would affect economics, and then I came across an essay by Weber. It's not as famous as the book *The Protestant Ethic and the Spirit of Capitalism*; it's called "The Protestant Sects and the Spirit of Capitalism." He was saying that one of the important impacts of Protestantism was actually increasing the degree of trust.

Weber tells the story of when he was traveling to the St. Louis World's Fair in 1898. He was on a train in the United States, sitting next to a salesman. They start talking about how the man traveled all over the place to sell things, and Weber asked him, "How do people trust you when you show up in a strange town"? The salesman said, "Well, I'm a Baptist, and I go to the Baptist Church; because I'm a fellow Baptist, the people there can deal with me, and they think that my products are going to be reliable." This led Weber to this insight that social trust was actually one of the impacts of the Reformation and of the sectarian nature of Protestantism in the United States. This gets subsequently labeled as social capital, meaning this ability of people to trust one another and work together collectively, not through a formal organization but just spontaneously. This really interested me and became my topic.

When I started thinking about this, the literature on social capital had started to appear. People like James Coleman and Robert Putnam had begun to write about the importance of social capital for politics.[2] And I thought maybe this is important in economics. So, I started reading across a lot of different literatures on Asia about how different China and Japan are regarding social capital. Japan has this tradition of social solidarity that started in the Tokugawa era. You learn how to work together in small villages for self-defense and to bring in the rice harvest. Whereas in China, you had larger and stronger families within a village, but these families regarded themselves as competitors. There was a high level of distrust outside the family. In Chinese society, the only way that you could get these people to work together was to have a strong state that forced them all to cooperate. That struck me as a really interesting pattern. I started looking for it in other societies, and that led to *Trust*, which focused on the importance of these social habits that then had a big effect in modernizing society. In Japan, because you had this tradition of being able to easily trust strangers, you had the development of large corporations very early on in the history of Japanese modernization. In China, on the other hand, the size of the companies remained small family businesses for a very long period of time, because in Chinese culture, it is just very hard to trust people who are not your relatives.

This structure deeply influences the economic system you have. There could be many similarities in countries that are not necessarily similar if you're looking for the mechanism that is important—that is, trusting of strangers. That was the interesting comparative part, because I talked about low-trust and high-trust societies. I didn't know anything about Latin America when I wrote that book, but when I started to spend more time in that region, it turned out to be a lot like China. People generally don't trust each other outside of the family. You see this even in things like domestic architecture. In both China and in Latin America, if you're a rich person, you don't have a fancy house on display for outsiders. Rather, you build your house all the way out to the perimeter of your property. All of the effort is made in making the inside beautiful. It's built around a private inner court because you don't want to excite the envy of your neighbors, nor do you want to attract the attention of the tax collector. Whereas in England, it's the opposite. You want to show everybody that you're well-to-do. You put your estate on a hill where everybody can see it. In America it's very similar, and that has to do with the degree of trust in society. In some societies, it's every family against every other family, a very competitive, distrustful situation, and that has deeply historical origins.

Education and economic growth underpin the success of liberal democracies, and you underline this in *Trust*. You are saying that some ethical habits clearly constitute virtues, but not all of them contribute to the formation of social capital. Can you elaborate on this?

Well, some virtues are individual, especially things like intellectual virtue. You can have a brilliant mathematician or a poet sitting all by yourself, and it doesn't really require any kind of social skill. In fact, there seems to be a negative correlation between certain kinds of cognitive skills and your social awareness. Human capital has to do with those skills and abilities that are possessed by individuals. If you get an education as an engineer, right? That's something that you have by yourself. But social capital really has to do with the relationships that you have with other people in your ability to work with them, share information, and behave in a trustworthy manner. That kind of ability requires other people.

But you mention the Mafia, for instance, and you say they have social capital.

Social capital is a morally neutral concept. You can have social capital in a criminal gang that is held together by a blood oath. Social capital's value depends on the uses to which it's put.

Trust is a key word in Norway. We are said to have very high levels of trust, and social scientists and historians are continuously discussing why, posing questions like "Have politics created trust, or is it the other way around?" There are scholars in Denmark and Sweden who have been looking into trust among Scandinavian Americans in the United States, and they have found that they still have greater trust, implying that they brought it with them from Scandinavia. What do you think?

It's important for people who think politics is everything to say trust was created because of good politics. But it is possible to think about it the opposite way. I think the causality goes in both directions, and in a high-trust society, because people trust each other, they like the state. It performs well, and people trust the state, and that is a virtuous circle. But in other societies, they don't trust the state, and the state doesn't work so well, and then they say, "Well, I'm justified in distrusting the state."

Do you think trust can be learned?

It's hard. There are instances where you've increased levels of trust. For example, Japan wasn't always a high-trust society, but they used mechanisms like lifetime employment to increase levels of trust after 1945. In the earlier part of the century you had strikes and labor demonstrations and social conflict. There was a deliberate effort by elites after

World War II to create mechanisms that would stabilize society. The Germans did the same thing. In Germany in the 1930s, you had communist labor unions responding to repression of worker's rights fighting bosses and fascist militias. After the war, they deliberately tried to create a social model where labor was intentionally incorporated into corporate decision-making. It can be done, but it's hard.

The Great Disruption Made Us Modern Individuals

The Great Disruption, from 1999, is about the social development of the United States and other Western countries. **You present four main reasons commonly used to explain why the disruption occurred: increasing poverty or income inequality, growing wealth, the modern welfare state, and "a broad cultural shift that included the decline of religion and the promotion of individualistic self-gratification over community obligation."[3] Can you explain why this transfer is important?**

Somebody once said that the entire discipline of sociology is built around the transition from a local small-scale village society to a modern urban society. That's the transition from *Gemeinschaft* to *Gesellschaft*. Explaining all of the consequences of that transition is really to explain modernization itself and how it's experienced by people.

I have spent a lot of time on this. I teach a course in comparative politics where we start out with the social dimensions of modernization, what it means for society to modernize. Modernization has to do with the development of individual opportunities. Modern societies are more pluralistic, there is much more choice, and identity becomes much more fluid. You need a greater diversity of people, you have much more freedom, but, on the other hand, you have much less social support. All of these things are part of what it means to live in a modern society.

The long-term decline in social indicators that I was describing in *The Great Disruption* looks different to me now. At the time I said social decline was due to the stresses caused by the shift from an industrial to a postindustrial society, and government policy didn't have much to do with it. That situation also looks a lot different today, after the financial crisis and the growth of populism. What happened in the United States was a long period of declining social trust among all Americans. Then it began to reverse itself, but only for people with a decent education. Since I published the book, it's really quite remarkable that a lot of the things I was talking about—the decline of trust, decline of families, growth of divorce rates, crime—all of that reversed, but only for upper-income educated people. It continued to get worse for people with just a high school education or less. African Americans were the first to be affected by the consequences of deindustrialization, but then it began to hit working-class whites who found themselves living in these highly disrupted communities. Back in the 1990s I wanted to blame all of this on changes in technology and the nature of work. Today, I think the structural economic drivers, like globalization and the elevated levels of inequality that it created, also have been important.

Like Society, Capitalism Changes over Time

Today not only liberal democracies are under attack; so is capitalism. Recently published books have titles like *The Future of Capitalism* and *Postcapitalism*.[4] Has capitalism become something very different from what Adam Smith described?

Well, I don't know if it's different. Capitalism has always gone through these periods where it was liberated from political constraints and then produced negative effects and had to be constrained again. A lot of late-nineteenth-century American capitalism looks like contemporary capitalism, where you have a great deal of inequality created in a relatively unregulated market. But, in fact, nineteenth-century capitalism was much more violent because the owners of companies were willing to hire armed men to shoot strikers and things like that. The level of social violence was quite high. It's a pendulum: You have social controls over capitalism that increase, and then that increases to the point where it stifles innovation and growth slows. Then you try to liberate it again, and it goes to the opposite extreme, too much cowboy capitalism.

The balance, then, is important—not too much restraint, no laissez-faire?

I have been thinking about Paul Collier's book *The Future of Capitalism*. In this book Collier questions the individualistic premises of mod-

ern economics and notes that human beings have a very strong com-
munal side that is ignored by contemporary theory. He argues that the
golden age of modern capitalism occurred when it was joined to social
democracy in Europe and created the modern European welfare state.

**The main ideas from *Trust* are built in a way that resembles the structure of
Origins of Political Order, going country by country and showing the underlying principles of how economic development and cultural and social
development are tied together. How do you see the ideas from *Trust* today?**

Empirically, things have changed. The Chinese can now build big companies, and the Japanese system looks a lot less successful because their
large companies ossified, became very rigid, and didn't really adapt. In
a certain sense, the Chinese small-company model was a more successful one in the long run.

**How do you see economic growth, technological development, and grow-
ing inequality in the years to come? Is work for all a utopia? Have you ever
thought about or written about universal basic income?**

I haven't written about it. I'm asked about it constantly. Well, it's not
going to work, for a couple of different reasons. One reason has to do
with whether you can afford it. I'm skeptical that you can, but the
other reason is deeper and has to do with dignity. People derive their
sense of self-worth from the fact that people are willing to pay them for
what they do in a labor market. But if you're just paid for being alive,
you have no basis for feeling proud and esteeming yourself. I forget in
which book it is, but somewhere Karl Marx writes about whether life
under communism would be like living in a place where all of your
productive needs were taken care of by a very efficient economy. And
he said that you could be a fisherman in the morning and a poet in the
evening, and it's kind of a vision that what you do to earn a living isn't
important. You should want to be a whole person. I think that this is
not how people actually behave. Their core work is really key to what
they think about themselves and their self-esteem.[5]

**As Branko Milanović wrote in his book *Capitalism Alone*, there are many
kinds of capitalism. Do you agree?**

Yes, you need to distinguish between capitalism per se, which is a very broad term that encompasses a lot of forms of economic organization, and a certain kind of extreme free market. Any capitalist system, if it's not linked to a democratic political system, is ultimately going to move in this kind of direction toward ever-increasing inequality because the market by itself is not sufficient to create a happy society.

You are talking about a restrained but meritocratic and liberal capitalism. How can it be restrained?

You need a political system that does things like provide social protections for people that redistribute income and guarantee access to health care and pensions. And if you neglect that, you're going to end up like we have in the United States, where many ordinary people are very disillusioned. You need to go back to an older conception of social democracy. This might maintain the legitimacy of a capitalist economic system and link it to a pretty broad set of social protections.

So how should we make sure that capitalism works to the benefit of us all?

If you could go back to this older sense that corporations also do have obligations to a wider circle of social actors than their shareholders, that would probably definitely help as well. And states are still really powerful. If you get the right political coalition together, I think you can get inequality under control.

* * *

Capitalism is closely connected to democracies and to technological development, but after the rise of China, debates about how capitalism works in autocracies are of current interest. Before we turn to China, our dialogue moves to human rights and what it is to be human.

Notes

1. Deirdre McCloskey is professor of economics and history and has written *Why Liberalism Works* (2019), and the economic, historical, and literary trilogy *The Bourgeois Era* (2006, 2010, 2016).

2. Putnam published *Bowling Alone* in 1995. Coleman published *Foundations of Social Theory* in 1990.

3. Fukuyama, *Great Disruption*, 65.

4. Collier, *Future of Capitalism*; and Mason, *Postcapitalism*.

5. Karl Marx wrote, in *German Ideology*, "to hunt in the morning, fish in the afternoon, look after the cattle in the evening and after supper criticize as much as I wish" (1846).

FOURTEEN

How Does Human Nature Shape Society?

One of Fukuyama's contributions to democratic theory has been his discussion of human nature. His arguments on how we collaborate and how we wish to be respected are biologically and psychologically anchored. This is why our understanding of human nature and what it means for our understanding of liberal democracy is important.

In *Our Posthuman Future*, which came just after *The Great Disruption*, Fukuyama starts with a gloomy prophecy: "I will argue, because human nature exists, it is a meaningful concept, and has provided a stable continuity to our experience as a species. It is, conjointly with religion, what defines our most basic values. Human nature shapes and constrains the possible kinds of political regimes, so a technology powerful enough to reshape what we are will have possibly malign consequences for liberal democracy and the nature of politics itself."[1] He continues to discuss human nature and biotechnology in an intriguing way. He even argues that biotech development is even scarier than what George Orwell described in *1984* as the "surveillance society."

Human Rights Are Grounded in Human Nature

Your first deep dive into human nature was *The Great Disruption*. The book you wrote after *The Great Disruption* was *Our Posthuman Future*. You once said that your interest in human nature dates from your time at Cornell with Allan Bloom.[2] How did he evoke your interest in human nature?

It wasn't actually Bloom. In classical political theories, natural right theory is important. If you look at Plato and Aristotle and their understanding of what a good life is, it is based on a distinction between nature and nurture. The things that are most deeply aligned with our natural desires and ends are what make us happy, and that's what structures politics and ethics and so forth. That's the beginning of this natural right tradition in Western thought, which says that rights are grounded in human nature. All of the early modern thinkers, like Thomas Hobbes, John Locke, and Jean-Jacques Rousseau, proceeded in exactly the same way. They had a different understanding of human nature, but they all said that what determines the priority of our values is what most accords with our deepest passions. Hobbes actually has, in one of the first chapters of the *Leviathan*, all this cataloguing of different human passions. He says the fear of violent death is the most important driver. That leads to the right to life and so forth. But Locke and Rousseau also have this start; that's why they talk about the state of nature, which is just a metaphor for human nature. It's an important strand in Western thought. That was just a speculation. If you believe that rights are grounded in nature, and if you can actually change nature, then you have thrown human rights out the window, in a certain sense, because the two are related.

What are human beings?

This question is one of the most basic but also the most tortured of all in the Western tradition. The economist's understanding of social cooperation is, I think, the silliest because they basically say that every one of us is born as a completely selfish individual. We simply calculate that it's in our self-interest to cooperate, and that's how you get cooperation. That's just the biggest bullshit ever. Human beings have individual desires, but they are social creatures from the start. It's clear that all of the mechanisms that facilitate cooperation are not rational ones. They are emotional ones. We get lonely if we don't have human contact. We care about the esteem of other people, and we want to act in ways that win the esteem, which usually means conforming to other people's expectations of you.

You have an entire species whose success compared to other species has been driven by the fact that they can cooperate socially. It's just that the nature of that cooperation has changed. The whole story in the political order books is how you evolve this cooperation from very small-scale kin groups to larger modern societies with hundreds of millions of people. The cooperation is built on this natural sociability, which, in turn, has to do with you recognizing another human being by this mechanism, even though those human beings are not your father or your son, but strangers.

Are we political animals, as Aristotle called us?

Aristotle said that, but he meant many things by that. I'm not in the end convinced that we're political animals in the sense that Aristotle said, because he really does have a teleological understanding of this. I would say we're social animals. We're just programmed to cooperate with one another, but Aristotle would go much further than that. He would say we're designed to live in a city that is diverse and allows a kind of high degree of intellectual flourishing. That's the way human societies have developed, but I'm not sure there was any teleology to this process. Aristotle really does have the sense that it's the development of one's full intellectual capacities to reason and philosophize that happens only in a certain kind of city. That's the kind of fulfillment of what it means to be a human being.

Let us turn to human rights. Where do they come from?

I discussed this in 2002 with Richard William Schulz, who was the head of Amnesty International.[3] I just made the simple observation that most modern defenders of human rights cannot articulate a theory as to why the current set of rights as understood in the West should be the ones that people have to adhere to. I asked him if he could say where human rights came from. And he said, "Oh, well, rights have just evolved over time." I asked him, "Okay, so the Chinese say, 'Well, we have a different understanding of rights, which is more collective than individual,' and they say that that's what's evolved in China. How do you go to the Chinese and then complain about the way that they are treating their citizens?" He didn't have a coherent answer to this question. I think that is indicative of the West today. Although we know where we came from in cultural terms, we no longer have any clear agreement about the moral foundations on which our current values are based. We don't have a coherent cultural narrative about where our most fundamental values come from, and that's very problematic. The American founding fathers had this idea that rights were natural, that they come out of a certain understanding of human nature, but very few theorists today would endorse that view.

We have been talking extensively about identity and dignity, and this is universal. How does this relate to human rights?

To the extent that there is a moral core to the modern idea of dignity, it really has to do with human agency. This is something that comes out of Christianity. Ultimately, what gives people equality in the eyes of God is that we are all moral agents who can make decisions about right and wrong. We no longer believe the religious version of it. We believe in a kind of secularized version, that, for example, we have the right to vote, we can make choices, we can "actualize" ourselves, and we should be able to make choices about who governs us. This is the idea that is embedded in the dignity language. That's how a lot of modern constitutions begin with the right to dignity, which I think is the right to agency.

How do you see that the role of human rights has evolved lately?

Well, it depends on how you define human rights and what scope they have. Despite the rise of populism and the rise of Trump, an American president who doesn't seem to care about global human rights at all, we've actually made a fair amount of progress over the last thirty years because there are institutions, there is international law. The importance of human rights has been elevated, and in that sense these new populists have not completely undermined the broader fabric of the international community, but it's certainly a big challenge right now.

Are human rights universal?

To the extent that they are universal, you would have to argue this is true in a historically contingent way. That is to say, all societies cross-culturally tend to evolve in similar ways and produce similar values over time as they modernize. No one in the West itself believed in our current understanding of human rights 150 years ago: they didn't believe that nonwhite people or women were full human beings endowed with equal rights; as little as 15 years ago few people believed in marriage equality. There is a certain cultural imperialism to the view that everyone in the world must sign up to the current Western understanding of human rights. The idea of universal recognition appears, as Hegel says, at a certain historical moment and only afterward becomes universalized because it is a solution to a universal human problem.

There are also some issues around the enforcement of universal rights. While in principle human rights apply universally, they are enforced by nations. And that means the nation still remains important in terms of the actual implementation of rights, and it means that human rights' authority is limited really by the scope of the nations' power. I'm not sure that you'd actually want to live in a world where any given country could enforce a human right in any other territory. The scope of enforcement power still needs to revolve around the nation and its territory, and that's a limitation. We can exert moral suasion and other kinds of pressures on countries to observe human rights, but the actual enforcement power is necessarily limited, and it should remain limited in principle.

Biotechnological Changes to Human Nature Affect Rights, Society, and Politics

In 1999 you said, "The open-ended character of modern natural science suggests that within the next couple of generations, biotechnology will give us tools that will allow us to accomplish what social engineers of the past failed to do. At that point, we will have definitively finished human history because we will have abolished human beings as such."[4] Let us talk about how you argue for a human nature and what is at stake.

I continue to believe that human rights are grounded in human nature. This is important because—as I said earlier—if you can change human nature, you're going to change the nature of rights. When you do that, you could manipulate people. We have this belief that fundamentally, at least in terms of our moral agency, we're all equal, but if you can actually breed different classes of people, that won't be necessarily true anymore. If you have genetically very distinct classes of people, the premise of treating them equally disappears.

You mention that you based the book *Our Posthuman Future* on an article called "Second Thoughts: The Last Man in a Bottle." Why did you choose this title?

Why the title . . . I was thinking a lot about biomedical technology and its effects on society and politics. It's not just editing your genes. It's also pharmacology, the use of drugs to control human behavior. And that's actually proceeded much further than people recognize. We use Ritalin and Prozac and Xanax and other drugs, amphetamines and selective serotonin reuptake inhibitors, to treat ADHD, depression, and other conditions. We're already trying to manipulate and achieve social control using drugs without being aware of these deep questions.

What are your main concerns, and are they still valid?

The major concerns about technology are coming true now very rapidly. At that time, it was just speculation that you could do this editing of human genes, but we now have CRISP-Cas9.[5] The technology is here, and it's effective, and the Chinese are going to be the first people to use it.

Why?

They just don't have the same moral constraints that people in the West do. Actually, I wrote an article about this once, which some people objected to as a cultural generalization, but I think it's still true that in the West you have this very sharp dichotomy between the human and the nonhuman. In the book of Genesis, God gives man dominion over the rest of nature. We accord much higher dignity to human beings than to the rest of the natural world. Whereas, in Asia, I think there is another perception of this relationship. It is more of a continuum. In the animistic religions of Asia, spirits are seen as pervading all things, including inanimate life. The dividing line between human and nonhuman is not that sharp. On the one hand, you have more respect for nonhuman nature but, on the other hand, less respect for the specificity of human dignity. Rates of abortion are higher in Asia, and there are many manifestations of this. I just think that, in the West, we're going to continue to have a lot of trouble with manipulating human beings. China is not a liberal democracy, and it is not clear that they will place the same regulatory constraints on germline engineering if they see some large national advantage to employing it.

Do you plan to follow up the arguments from this book?

I wrote that book when I was on George W. Bush's Bioethics Council. I had a concrete work plan, which was to try to advocate for a regulatory system to control this kind of biomedical technology. It got nowhere, so I just gave up. But maybe at a later point I will come back to it.

Human Nature Is Biologically and Socially Constructed

What will happen if we stop being human?

Well, I don't know. I mean it's really hard to predict. You can imagine all sorts of outcomes that will look very bad from our perspective today, where you have a much greater willingness to manipulate the behavior of other people coupled with a greater ability to do so. It can happen in the West as well.

Human equality and the human capacity for moral choices can be altered, according to your arguments in *Our Posthuman Future*.

One of the issues I discuss in that book is the issue of life extension. This is something that many Silicon Valley billionaires are pouring a lot of money into. I, on the other hand, think that it's a terrible idea. There's a good reason why we die and why we have generational turnover. If people could live to be two hundred years old, the rate of social change and adaptation, which is often brought about by generational turnover, will slow dramatically. Not to speak about the consequences for global population and resources.

You further write, "It is my view that the common understanding of the naturalistic fallacy is itself fallacious and that there is a desperate need for philosophy to return to the pre-Kantian tradition that grounds rights and morality in nature."[6] As I read you, you are saying that academic philosophers and political/legal theorists are assuming many things about human beings that are based in human nature, but their argument is that their

ethical theories are not based in human nature. Can you explain? It seems to me that you do not have much sympathy for utilitarianism. Is that right?

In the West, moral philosophy has evolved in a way that dramatically privileges individual agency. As I wrote in *Identity*, agency is the human characteristic at the core of our current understanding of equal rights and human dignity. But while people have agency, it is not unlimited. It is limited, in the first place, by the fact that we live in large societies and need to cooperate with other human beings. But it is also limited by the fact that we are not just minds making choices but have bodies as well.

This tension is mostly clearly visible in gender politics today. Modern feminism was driven by the idea that women are equal to men in all respects and therefore should be treated the same juridically and socially and should expect equal outcomes in terms of income, employment, and the like. This is, of course, a very desirable goal. There has been a strong view among many feminists that existing disparities are entirely the result of gender discrimination and are not related to biological differences between men and women.

Now, it is certainly the case that many things we once thought were biologically grounded were in fact socially constructed. Women have massively moved into the workforce and are doing jobs, like fighting in combat units, that people a generation or two ago thought would not be possible. It is clear that, for certain individuals, there is a weak connection between biological sex and gender. But we still have bodies and biologies. The idea that there is *no* connection between biological sex and gender over the population as a whole is absurd. What you have for many characteristics are overlapping normal distributions with different centers.

So, while human agency is at the core of our understanding of what it means to be human, a full account of human nature needs to take account of how that capacity for choice interacts with the biological substrate that we share. We are free, but we are also limited in that freedom by our social conditions and by our own human natures.

And what about the Kantian tradition?

So there's a category of moral reasoning that is sometimes called deontological. This starts with Immanuel Kant. Kant developed moral rules without regard to the actual nature of people, based on no prior knowledge of the actual situation of the creatures that you're dealing with. In a way, the emphasis on human beings as agents without bodies and natures can be traced back to Kant. That's never really struck me as a very realistic moral strategy because a lot of our moral reasoning is based on context, on a very intimate knowledge of the way people are and act, the societies in which they are embedded, and so forth. This view necessarily leads to a certain degree of relativism because different cultures really do prize different things, and you can't derive any of those from abstract moral thinking. Although I do believe that there is a kind of universal human nature that puts certain boundaries around moral rules, there still is a lot of cultural variation within them.

Finally, am I right in assuming that you have a small preference for the two Greeks, Aristotle and Plato?

Well, I think Aristotle's *Nicomachean Ethics* has a richer understanding of morality than Kant's deontological framework or the Anglo-American utilitarian tradition. The problem with utilitarianism is that it just places a kind of low threshold on what we strive for as human beings, that is, simply maximizing utility, like the economists say.

* * *

The question of human rights is also a core issue when it comes to China. Does the main thesis of liberal democracies, the value of human rights, also hold for China? China is not a liberal democracy and has experienced huge economic growth during the past thirty years.

Notes

1. Fukuyama, *Our Posthuman Future*, 7.
2. "History's Pallbearer."
3. Schulz, Fox, Fukuyama, "Ground and Nature of Human Rights."
4. "Second Thoughts."
5. CRISP-Cas9 is a method for genome editing. CRISP is short for "clusters of regularly interspaced short palindromic repeats."
6. Fukuyama, *Our Posthuman Future*, 112.

FIFTEEN

Is China a Serious Contender to Liberal Democracy?

In 1989 Fukuyama thought it was too early to conclude that strong states were a thing of the past because even if communism as a totalitarian system was demolished, it could be replaced by new nationalistic, authoritarian political systems or perhaps fascism in a Russian or Serbian variant. These regimes could be equally challenging to democracies, as the Soviet Union was earlier. He believed the largest and probably the most likely contestant would come from the most successful autocracy—China. "The End of History?" was written before the Tiananmen Square protests, and the Chinese position has since dramatically strengthened, both economically and politically.

Typically in countries that have a large middle class, one can also be quite sure of finding political freedom and economic growth. Studies in political science and economics have shown that a large middle class is an important indicator of how a society will develop politically. A strong middle class with economic and educational resources is more prone to want property rights and democratic accountability.

The Chinese Model

Are China and the Chinese model a serious contender to liberal democracy?

The interesting debate is if there is a real alternative to liberal democracy. But like I've said consistently ever since I wrote *The End of History*, the single most serious challenge to the idea of the end of history thesis is China because it's a country that's shown itself able to modernize in a very effective way, to use science and technology, to increase economic output, but it has done that under authoritarian conditions. And if

China continues to rise the next thirty years, there is indeed an alternative model to liberal democracy that looks pretty effective.

Is it possible for other countries to adapt the Chinese model?

I don't think China has a readily exportable model. China draws on a very long history of meritocratic centralized bureaucracy and a strong cultural emphasis on education. Other countries in East Asia under its cultural influence, like Japan, Korea, and Taiwan, have done well because of that inheritance. China and these other countries established a strong sense of national identity long before they began to modernize. But if you don't have these Confucian traditions, it's not so easy to adopt the model. If you look at sub-Saharan Africa's would-be "developmental states," like Rwanda and Ethiopia, they are a long way from having achieved the kind of institutionalized autocracy that China possesses. They also have underlying ethnic cleavages that China does not have to deal with.

Chinese students are flooding into universities abroad. What does this mean, and do you have any experience with Chinese students?

A lot of American universities have become so dependent on Chinese students that if you try to invite a speaker who has criticized China, all of a sudden you get a petition from the Chinese Students Association that protests. In fact, a friend of mine experienced this a while ago. They tried to invite a speaker on Tibet, and they got a petition of fifteen thousand signatories who protested, saying not only that they could not invite this person but that they should fire the professor that invited this speaker. China has been able to extend its influence into the heart of Western societies in what has been labeled an exercise of "sharp power," and we have to defend Western values and basic liberal values against it.

We have been talking about technology, and China has the size to exploit big data in ways that are unprecedented. In the West, there have been discussions about the influence of Huawei Technology Company. What are your thoughts?

I support public investment in Ericsson and other potential alternatives because you need an alternative to Huawei. The Chinese are trying to create surveillance that no totalitarian country has ever been able to do on this scale previously. They can follow every single transaction and track where you are physically. They have the technological means to punish you for these very small deviations. The Chinese are a bigger challenge than Russia in the long run simply because they are so big and powerful. This trend will obviously be accelerated as a result of the COVID-19 pandemic. A million Muslims were put in camps and are living under this extraordinary surveillance, and it is deeply disturbing. Very few other countries wanted to make a fuss about this, including many Muslim countries, for fear of angering China. The European Union now is completely blocked from saying anything negative about China because just one country like Hungary or Greece can say, "No we're not going to offend China because we've got an infrastructure project at their funding," and that's it.

Talking about infrastructure, the Chinese are building infrastructure, like the Belt and Road Initiative, and buying up valuable natural resources in many countries, while not asking or being asked about human rights. Do you think China will continue to be a political system that at least non-Western countries admire and try to emulate?

Not entirely. We should not let ourselves off the hook too easily, because part of the reason China seems like an attractive alternative to the West is that the West has really not been good at providing developing countries with the kinds of things like roads, electricity, and ports that they really need to develop. The Chinese are very good at providing infrastructure. There's been a big failure on the part of Western countries to do that. Infrastructure is necessary for economic growth. Somehow seeing this as simply an evil plot by the Chinese is wrong. There are many projects that have actually been beneficial both to China and to the country that's received the project, but the Chinese have not been very careful in their investments. A lot of times they've invested more for political purposes than because it has made economic sense. It's very hard for Western countries to tell an African country that desperately needs an electrical grid that you shouldn't take this Chinese offer just because they don't meet Western standards for safeguards. As a consequence, countries get over-indebted, and they can't repay their loans, and that leads to a big crisis.

As long as the Chinese have economic resources, they will probably continue to do what they have been doing. Other countries are still going to want Chinese investment because, like I said, it's a big failure on the part of the West not to be able to provide this.

When Economic Growth Does Not Create a Surge for Liberal Democracy

The Scientific Revolution and technological development have for the past four hundred years been closely connected to the emergence of a modern economy and rising living standards. Is economic development a prerequisite for liberal democracy?

Although some countries have managed to reach the end of history in my terms, it may be argued that this is not going to be at all universal. By this view, the end of history is only going to be the property of a very small handful of countries, and the vast majority of poor countries today are going to stay poor, or they're simply not going to adopt modern institutions. There are different reasons given for this. It used to be a kind of Marxist argument that the current global system was holding these countries in permanent dependency. I don't think that's right, but it could be that for cultural or historical reasons of historical legacies you're going to get countries that simply will never turn into modern industrialized societies. There are some actual versions of Marx's original interpretation that now seem to me to make more sense than they did a few decades ago. For example, he talked about the crisis of overproduction, where capitalism would become so efficient that it produced more goods than were demanded by an increasingly impoverished population. According to John Hobson and Vladimir Lenin, they then turned to imperialism because capitalists constantly needed new markets for the products they were producing so efficiently.

This has come true in a certain way. If you look around the world today, we don't need any more car factories, we don't need any more steel factories, because the existing producers, particularly in China, are so efficient that they're producing more than can be consumed. The actual problem is a lack of demand, and that's part of the reason that interest rates have been so low for the last two decades. There just aren't that many new productive opportunities. It is the result of inequality, where the largest rewards go to a narrow elite at the top, who can't generate adequate demand on their own to keep the machine running. This has big implications for developing countries. It means that a lot of countries that would like to replicate South Korea's or Japan's export-driven growth model are not going to be able to do so because the market is not there: there would be no buyers for their products.

In *Falling Behind*, you mention in your conclusion that, fundamentally, it is probably a weak rule of law that hinders Latin American development. China works, Latin America does not—do you have some thoughts today about this a decade later?

I would say that the rule of law and a modern state really overlap to a great extent. It's hard to know which is due to state weakness and which is due to lack of the rule of law. For example, the rule of law doesn't mean anything unless it can be enforced. It's enforced by a state and, ideally, it's enforced in an impersonal manner. That's really what's missing in Latin America. So you have the growth of all these narco-mafias that the state really can't control; they have taken over some states entirely in Venezuela and certain state governments in Mexico. These states simply can't enforce basic rules. They can't protect their populations from gang violence murder.

Yes, but China?

Well, China does have a very effective system. It's got a very strong state coming out of its own historical tradition. It's a more competent state than most authoritarian dictatorships because it's highly institutionalized. At the lower levels, it's very meritocratic. They don't promote people that don't have the proper background. You have patronage in the Chinese system, but that tends to happen only at the higher levels where you've got different factions within the Communist Party that are competing against each other. But at lower levels of the party and government, there is a real bureaucracy. They've handled that process pretty competently, given how large China is and how difficult it is to administer a complex country like that. The question, really, is how stable it is going to be in the future. They've got a lot of problems having to do with information and dealing with rapid social change and so forth.

The economic miracle has given China muscle internationally, but it may have postponed the "normal" wish of a middle class to demand political participation. Will this last? The big question is, Will China ever become a liberal democracy? And if not, why?

Well, we don't know. The theory says that a rising middle class will demand more participation, and so far that does not seem to have happened in China. This is standard modernization theory: as you get richer, you get a middle class that wants more political participation. They want to protect their property rights and so forth. They're already at a level of per capita income where that should have kicked in. China is basically where Taiwan and South Korea were in the 1980s, when they had a middle class that led to democracy in those two countries. I don't see much evidence that it's happening in China. And is that because in Chinese culture you just don't have this kind of demand, or is it because there are just other circumstances that haven't made the time ripe? Under different circumstances—like, let's say, a prolonged period of economic stagnation—then maybe people will start demanding that. We just don't know.

China has a quite large middle class, but they also have an aging population, and the standard of living has increased substantially. Have we over-estimated the middle-class wish for political influence and participation? Does the fact of a shrinking work force in the years to come play any role in political development?

China has defied the expectations that the middle class will press for democracy on this ladder. It's really hard to know the impact of an aging population. Demography is not only a problem for China. Virtually every developed country is facing an aging population to a greater or lesser extent. This is a problem in Europe, especially in the southern parts, and a big problem in the democratic parts of Asia—Japan, South Korea, and Taiwan. All actually have extremely low birth rates, and this is also the case in China, but at least they still have a lot of momentum given its younger population, although in another fifteen years it will go down.

Chinese Ambitions Are Economic, Not Liberal

Early in the summer of 2019 a relatively insignificant legislative proposal sparked protests in Hong Kong that are still ongoing. What are your views on Hong Kong and the possible long-term outcome? More generally, can you comment on China's future global ambitions?

China is behaving just the way every other rising great power has behaved as they get more powerful. In the last ten years, and especially since Xi Jinping has come to power, they've been much more assertive in foreign policy. Their militarization of the islands in the South China Sea and the Belt and Road Initiative are examples. The Belt and Road Initiative is clearly serving Chinese foreign policy interests. When it comes to Hong Kong, events have shown that Hong Kong has a different culture than China. Essentially, the protesters are saying, "We don't want to regard ourselves just as loyal Chinese citizens." Beijing has to take account of that. It's going to be very hard to absorb Hong Kong the way the Chinese Communist Party absorbed other parts of the mainland. They appear to be using the COVID-19 epidemic as an excuse to tighten their control over Hong Kong. They're also concerned about their international reputation. But it is not certain that China needs a very strong, very prosperous Hong Kong for the next twenty years in the way it has in the past.

Can the world learn to live with an aggressive China?

No, that's going to continue to be a big problem, because China is reshaping the whole global architecture. I've felt for a long time that the biggest long-term threat to global order is China, not Russia or jihadists in the Middle East, because they're so much more powerful. The Chinese Communist Party rules a big, rich, powerful country. The reason that jihadists shoot up people in a theater or a café is that they don't have any other ways of affecting anything. It's dramatic but also pathetic. The Chinese will be larger than the United States economically if they don't hit a really big roadblock. That's going to happen in another decade.

Will China attack Taiwan?

That possibility is a real one. Most people, including a lot of people in Taiwan, just don't take that seriously, but it is a real possibility, and I have thought for some time that the prospect of actual military conflict in East Asia is much higher than the global business community thinks. China's ambitions expand the more powerful they are, and we've already seen that in the South China Sea where they have militarized these islands.

In 2018 you said of China,

> On domestic issues, there really is a liberal middle class. But on foreign policy, it's really different. There's a huge amount of nationalism and a lot of pent-up resentment about China not being treated fairly and respectfully. A democratic China could actually be more nationalist in certain ways because the politicians are going to have to compete for votes, and one of the ways of getting them is by demagoguing on nationalist issues.[1]

Will China be the dominant power in the long run?

I don't think that China will ever occupy the kind of hegemonic position that the United States has had.

In 2010 you were asked if you disagreed with Chinese intellectuals who argued that in the future, with a strong China, the world would be "tired" of the "debate over autocracy versus democracy" and would "yield to a more pragmatic debate over good governance versus bad governance."[2] Do you still disagree?

Democracy and individual rights are valuable not just as a means to good governance and economic growth; they are important in themselves as the way that democratic societies recognize the agency and dignity of their citizens. People in the West are not going to give this up for some abstraction called "good governance."

The Problem with Strong Leaders and the Weakness of Authoritarian Regimes

In the *Journal of Democracy*, Fukuyama points out, "It is the failure to establish modern, well-governed states that has been the Achilles heel of recent democratic transitions."[3] China has recently granted president Xi Jinping his position for life. Transitions are one of the key issues for a political order without rules for succession and without the possibility of removing a leader or a politician.

In 2011 you were challenged by professor Zhang Weiwei in a dialogue about the China Model, and you had to defend your views on China.[4] What are your thoughts on the problem of succession for the China Model?

Succession is a big problem for all authoritarian regimes. One of the characteristics that made the Chinese party state stand out among authoritarian regimes is the fact that it had become much more institutionalized after 1978. That means it had developed rules. There were rules on mandatory retirement, there were rules about succession, with ten-year term limits. There were rules governing the standing committee of the Politburo and how they were to manage their affairs. Xi Jinping has undermined a lot of those. They have become deinstitutionalized, which I think is never a good thing.

Why do you think he did it?

Who knows? He clearly thinks that he's indispensable. Ten years isn't going to be enough time to do the things that he wants to do. Who knows what his real motives are? But Xi has enemies; he has pissed off a lot of people within the party, so he can't just retire.

One issue is leadership succession; another is how an authoritarian country tackles a crisis. One such threat was the coronavirus that struck China before Christmas in 2019.

In theory China's political system has many weaknesses. You can see in this coronavirus case an attempt to control everything from the top. In a crisis like this, that attempt has terrible effects because people don't want to be honest about what they see right in front of them. Leaders were suppressing local professionals' warnings about how bad it was, and then this first doctor died of the virus.

On the other hand, the Chinese state has a lot of enforcement power and has been able to get to a point where the pandemic is under control, and it can reopen its economy. This comes at a huge cost in terms of people's rights, and democratic countries like South Korea have been able to achieve even better results with less authoritarian means. Nonetheless, China's performance in the COVID-19 crisis looks pretty disciplined compared to the shambolic US response.

This is one example of a serious virus, and we don't know how this will continue, but generally how can these kinds of threats destabilize China?

It all depends on how long such a threat will last. If they eventually get it under control, it will not have any impact, but if it really gets out of hand, and the economy slows down for an extended period of time, you could see some challenges to the leadership emerging. However, I believe that it is a big mistake to count on these weaknesses playing out in a way that will significantly slow China's rise. For planning purposes, we have to assume that China will continue to grow significantly faster than us for a number of years up to the point that China will have the largest economy in the world quite clearly and where their per capita gross domestic product will start to converge with that of Europe and the United States.

In any event, people's reactions may be determined more by relative than absolute performance. Many people in China were shocked at how badly a number of democratic countries handled the COVID-19 crisis, including Italy, Spain, and the United States. This has tamped down the early domestic criticisms of China's own response.

One of the greatest advantages we still have over China must be that we can replace bad leaders.

Yes, one of the big advantages of having a real liberal democracy as opposed to just a liberal order is that if a ruling elite really screws up, you've got a way of getting rid of them. That's not something we should want to give up very easily.

Notes

1. "Modi Is Pretty Impressive."
2. Fukuyama, "'End of History' 20 Years Later."
3. Fukuyama, "Why Is Democracy Performing So Poorly?," 12.
4. Fukuyama, "The China Model."

SIXTEEN

Are We Experiencing a Clash of Civilizations?

We are coming back to the controversies between Fukuyama and Samuel Huntington. The famous controversy between them came with the publication of Huntington's *The Clash of Civilizations*, in which he divides the world into seven or eight civilizations based on cultural differences. Huntington's position is that he sees culture and identity as the basis for current and future conflicts that will arise between these civilizations. In Huntington's view, there are no universal values, and different value systems will therefore clash and create unrest and conflicts.[1] Commemorating *The End of History* in 2010, Fukuyama wrote, "The differences between Huntington and me have been somewhat overstated. I wrote a book called *Trust* in which I argue that culture is one of the key factors that determines economic success and the possibilities of prosperity. So, I don't deny the critical role of culture. But, overall, the question is whether cultural characteristics are so rooted that there is no chance of universal values or a convergence of values. That is where I disagree."[2]

Religion as Cultural Difference

The controversy between you and Huntington, as I understand it, is about the understanding of culture and religion and how this affects political development. Are the institutions and values of the liberal West universal, or are they, as Huntington said, merely the outgrowth of cultural habits of Northern Europe?

In a way, that's the most serious challenge to the end of history hypothesis. What I have argued in the past was that, obviously, liberal values are not universal; rather, they developed contingently over time. Even in the West, they weren't practiced for centuries. Modern liberalism appears in Europe for the first time in the seventeenth century in response to the wars of religion following the Reformation. To the extent that there's a kind of universal history, it has to be based on a historical assertion that countries modernize and that they go through certain familiar stages that do not depend on culture. That's what I was trying to explain in my two political order books. If you take a really long view of human history, there has been this remarkable progression through different historical stages. You go through hunter-gatherer societies, then band level, then tribal societies, and these get replicated in almost every part of the world. You get state-level societies, and then you get societies that begin adding law and democratic accountability. There are clearly universal patterns of development. In East Asia, if you look at the social changes that have gone on as they've gotten richer, these nations replicate what's happened in Europe: there's urbanization, greater levels of education, greater mobility. In short, modernization. The only part that hasn't been replicated at high levels of economic development is democracy, although the latter did appear in Japan, South Korea, and Taiwan.

Let's say we replace liberal universal democracy or liberal democracy by just saying "modernization processes," then you are saying that they look similar.

Yes, they look very similar.

I interpret Huntington as more pessimistic than you, am I right?

Yes, he believed that, essentially, liberal democracy was just the unique product of the Western experience.

And other countries weren't going to be liberal democracies. Was he brushing liberal democracy off in a way?

Well, not brushing it off. He thinks it's the best system, but it's not a universal one. And so, therefore, it's really only going to flourish in countries that have this kind of Western cultural heritage.

In 2018 you stated, "I might as well begin by tackling at the outset the issue of how we're doing vis-à-vis one another. At the moment, it looks like Huntington is winning."[3] And you add, "The jury is still out on these issues." That was a while ago. How do you see this debate you had with him today?

Right from the beginning, it seemed to me that he didn't recognize certain integrative forces. These forces look weaker now that globalization has produced this kind of backlash, but it's not clear to me that you can ever completely reverse that process. What I said in that article was that his unit of analysis was wrong. I always admitted that culture was or remained important, but his understanding of culture was defined basically by religious heritage and their big units—Confucian or Western Christian or Hindu societies. I think the way identity has played out is that it's sometimes based broadly on a large cultural unit. But the actual identities that matter to people are always much smaller than that and much more fluid. They don't necessarily really determine the way that countries are going to develop. Contemporary Japanese and Koreans do not feel any sense of mutual solidarity because they're supposedly all part of a single "Confucian" cultural group.

To me, it seems that Huntington had a more static view, that values—and cultures, to a lesser extent—cannot adapt, change, or influence each other. Whereas you have, in my opinion, a more dynamic view. Cultures and values are open to change. The crux of the matter is how influence works, who influences whom, and in what direction that takes us.

Huntington did not believe that universal values exist. Each of the world's big civilizations, according to him, was built around a certain set of shared values whose roots lie in a complex historical past and were ultimately incommensurate with one another.

He also argued that cultural influence is really a matter of power. As long as the United States looks like it is the most powerful country in the world, people want to imitate its model; and once China begins to eclipse the United States, then China's model will be more popular. So that's one possible outcome. The question, then, is how likely it is that a China model is actually going to dominate global politics. I have some doubts, but I'd be the first to say that I have no idea what's going to happen.

Huntington argues that some societies are too strongly attached to their cultural values and that those values are not compatible with a liberal democratic political order, which will prevent them from modernizing or will make them create political systems that are different. Will his argument hold?

You need a more nuanced position because there's no question that cultural values affect the ability to modernize, but, on the other hand, cultural values also change. The question is, Will they change sufficiently to permit modernization? Seventy-five or a hundred years ago, most Western observers thought that East Asia would never modernize. Yet it did, and so anybody who confidently says that a certain society has a set of cultural values that will make it impossible to modernize should be a little careful in making that assertion.

What would Huntington say today?

Well, I think he would probably say he was basically right since the rise of religion continues to be really important. He spent the last decade of his life looking at the impact of religion on politics across the world.

Do you agree that religion is important?

It's important, but I don't think it determines outcomes, and a lot of the important divisions actually come within these religious groups. Islam, for instance, is undergoing a civil war between its Shiite and Sunni branches. There are parts of the world where religion is just not that important. In East Asia, they really don't have anything like religion in the Western or Islamic or Hindu sense, as a highly organized institutionalized body of rules and values emanating from belief in a transcendent deity.

If culture and religion define a country and that country happened to be a liberal democracy, then the argument that liberal democracies build on certain universal principles would not be valid. Does your disagreement come down to this? Or do you think that it is also a question of perspective and time? That over time, you may be right, things are not static? As you have said, "You'd never have any cultural progress in the world if people weren't appropriating from other people's cultures."[4]

That's correct. Religion may lie in the background of the new populist movements in Europe and the United States, but they are powered by plenty of old-fashioned forces like nationalism, ethnicity, race, economic inequality, and shared historical memory. In a way, what Huntington said was relevant to the current populist revolt because, for elites, there was a belief that they had somehow transcended culture. This is what Huntington referred to as "Davos Man." If you look across Europe, there is a whole layer of young people who are quite cosmopolitan and move around and don't care that much about what country they grew up in. But many people aren't that way, and they remain rooted in their societies. They don't move, and they are much more attached to traditional values. That's actually become the major fault line in Brexit and in a lot of the current debates over the future of Europe. But in the long run, it's the more educated mobile people that are going to create most of the wealth. Things have been moving in this direction pretty steadily in terms of how many people get an education. People move into towns or cities, and they go to institutions of higher education, and they create wealth. That is what happens in this modernization process.

Islamism and Democratic Values

In *The End of History* Fukuyama writes the following: "Orthodox Judaism and fundamentalist Islam, by contrast, are totalistic religions which seek to regulate every aspect of human life, both public and private, including the realm of politics. These religions may be compatible with democracy—Islam, in particular, establishes no less than Christianity the principle of universal human equality—but they are very hard to reconcile with liberalism and the recognition of universal rights, particularly freedom of conscience or religion."[5]

I have this quote from an interview you gave where you say, "I think that some forms of Islamism are actually driven by a desire for recognition, in which case the inner dignity is that of being a Muslim and that of feeling that Muslims are being persecuted or killed or repressed in different parts of the world and the dignity you seek, as a Muslim is to be part of this umma is given respect by non-Muslims. That's a form of dignity politics also."[6] This is scary stuff. In a way Islamism is an example of a successful

identity project, but at the same time it is violent, polarizing, and incompatible with liberal democracies. ISIS or Daesh has lost the territory necessary to form a nation state, but ISIS still exists. Is it different from earlier radical movements?

Well, it's more extreme. Extremism is fed by Saudi Arabia. Basically, after the grand mosque attack in 1989, the Saudis started to make a big effort to export Salafism, this ultraconservative form of Islam. Really, the problem is not with Islam because there are much more liberal and tolerant versions of Islam than Salafism. I really think Saudi Arabia is the source of this problem, and they are feeding on this special form, which is different.

And more violent?

The violence is one thing, but more generally the Saudi version of Islam is just not in line with democratic values in terms of attitudes toward women, toward gays and lesbians, toward Jews. They don't believe in fundamental equality.

A fundamental question is whether we will see a "liberal" Islam in the future—what are your thoughts?

I hope it happens. But the Saudis have a lot of money, so their support for conservative Islam can go on for some time. You have other countries with huge Muslim populations. But Muslim societies like Indonesia have been getting much more radical over the last few years.

How do you see fundamentalist Islam today after the Arab Spring, the civil war in Syria, and recent development in the Middle East?

The reason that the Arab Spring didn't result in democracy, except in Tunisia, was first the appearance of nondemocratic Islamist parties and then a backlash against them as in Egypt. Only in Tunisia did you have a more moderate Islamist party, Ennahda, that was willing to play by democratic rules.

We should look at Islamism as politics, not religious worship?

Islamism by definition is the political expression of the religion Islam. I would argue that Islamism, radical Islamism, is only partly a religious phenomenon. There are true believers, pious Muslims, who feel up-rooted from their surroundings. A lot of second- and third-generation European Muslims find themselves in this difficult cultural situation where they made a break with the religious traditions of their parents or grandparents, but they don't feel accepted by the European society in which they settled. As a political movement, a lot of what drives that is also a quest for recognition and identity. If you listen to the rhetoric of Osama bin Laden, and many different radical leaders, they say something very similar: We are part of a despised group. We are proud Muslims. We are not respected in the countries that are the dominant in the world, the United States and Germany. We are treated unfairly in our own countries, and we as Muslims need to show the world that we can fight back. The way you fight back is by joining this global umma that stretches all the way around the world and gives Muslims dignity.

Is this Islamism a kind of nationalism?

Religion and nationalism are alternative forms of modern identity that are used by political entrepreneurs to gain power. That's the way you get people to follow you. Identity is driving a lot of modern politics.

State Control of Migration Levels

What do you think of philosophical cosmopolitan arguments in favor of human rights to international freedom of movement?

I think it's a very one-sided argument because it doesn't take politics into account. I mean, you don't have a global state that can enforce global human rights. And, therefore, you have to rely on existing states to do enforcement. They have limited authority, and they also have political interests other than global human rights that they have to defend. Some people in the global human rights movement have asserted that there's a universal right to migration. I think that's a crazy idea. That's politically going to be extremely destabilizing.

So, are they only naive in their idealism and neglect for actual politics, or is there also something normatively wrong with their ideas? That is, in your

view, does liberal democracy come with an inherently restrictive element of a "demos" bounded along some identity marker?

Yes, I think it has to be. The right to international migration is normatively wrong because a democracy means sovereignty of the people, and if you can't define who the people are, you can't have a democracy. Therefore, if anyone has a right to join your community and become part of the people regardless of whether the people want that or not, such a situation just makes democracy incoherent.

Are considerations of culture valid reasons for restricting immigration from states that are far from liberal democracies? Is migration a domain where the universal values that ground liberal democracy, on the one hand, and the social cohesion / trust that makes liberal democracy work, on the other, pull in different directions? If so, how do we resolve the tension?

It depends what you mean by culture. Today it is unacceptable to define culture in ethnic or religious terms, because most modern societies are highly diverse in terms of ethnicity and religion. However, liberal democracy has its own cultural norms, and it is perfectly legitimate for such a society to demand that newcomers adopt those values.

There is a separate normative question about what obligations we have to needy people outside our society. Just as an individual does not have an obligation to give away all of his or her resources to poor people in their own country, a country doesn't have an unlimited obligation to take care of people who are oppressed or needy around the world. You do have to start with the concern for your own population first, and then, if you're rich enough, you can try to help other people. But there's not a necessary or an unlimited obligation to help other people.

You have written that you think that the state is the largest desirable political unit.

Well, that's one problem. It's also the case that the theory of democracy assumes a bounded state. It really doesn't work if there are no limits to who's part of the state.

But could one not make the argument that global migration demonstrates the need for a larger, supranational institution to coordinate a response to

global poverty, oppression, and exploitation? Such an institution, one could argue, is necessary because the state system is currently incapable of securing the rights that liberal democracy is in place to protect.

Obviously, the European Union creates another level of authority, and that has confused the issues. But the real power in Europe still remains at a national level. We see this today with regard to decisions on foreign and fiscal policy, where individual member states still retain substantial veto power.

Assimilation and Multiculturalism

Multiculturalism is the dominant cultural position in the West and contains the view that immigrants should be able keep their habits, culture, and values. Is this problematic?

Most Western societies up through the middle of the twentieth century were basically Christian societies in which you had a common religious set of cultural values that defined morality and the way that people saw the world. These societies began to secularize in the late nineteenth and twentieth centuries. In some cases, those religious ideas were replaced by ideology and Marxism and other kinds of systematic belief systems, but essentially by the time you get to the second half of the twentieth century, there is no overarching set of values that really unites Western societies. Multiculturalism is just an expression of that kind of moral incoherence. Individual autonomy is interpreted to mean that people get to make up their own value systems. You try to celebrate multiculturalism instead of forcing some kind of conformity, and that leads to larger problems, and you can't really articulate what is the moral basis of your own societies. But you need common value systems in order for people to be able to cooperate with one another.

If liberal democracy is, in part, supposed to guarantee that the state allows its citizens to "pursue their own conceptions of the good," to use John Rawls's phrase, is there then a danger of demanding too much integration?[7]

No, the biggest challenge is going to be dealing with Muslim minorities. The consensus really had to do with the fact that countries were ethnically and religiously very homogeneous. And now you have a substantial population that is really quite different. The question is

the same faced by many European countries: Will an immigrant minority eventually integrate into a broader national identity, or will it
become a kind of parallel society that exists in the country but never
really feels part of it? The latter, I think, would be a very bad outcome.
This is what politics looks like in places like the Balkans or the Middle
East. If you have the opportunity to assimilate religious and ethnic
minorities into a broader liberal and democratic culture, you should
opt for that.

**In a previous interview, you called for "the assimilation of immigrants into
a culture that isn't afraid to say what it values and what it rejects."[8] To many,
assimilation has for a long time been a taboo, and "integration" has been
the politically correct term to use. Immigrants should be able to keep their
culture, practices, and values and only be expected to respect the rule of law
and basic democratic rights. Assimilation means becoming part of a nation
and identifying with the country on a deeper level. How do you see the difference, and why is assimilation important?**

I had been thinking about this issue after I had spent a lot of time visiting the Netherlands and other European countries that were wres-
tling with the aftermath of September 11. I realized they had Muslim
communities that were not very well integrated into their societies,
and they were trying to figure out how to handle integration. This
integration policy was intriguing and interesting to study. In America,
assimilation doesn't have the same kind of negative connotation. To
me, it just means accepting some of the basic characteristics of the
culture, the language, and a lot of the habits and so forth.

* * *

In 2018 Fukuyama commemorated the twenty-fifth anniversary of the
publication of *The Clash of Civilizations*. After the publication of *Who
Are We?* Huntington was accused of being an anti-immigrant racist.
Fukuyama attempted to nuance the common view of Huntington and
argues that his own view is correct:

> The "Anglo-Protestant" settlers of North America contributed to
> the country's success not because of their ethnicity, but because
> of the cultural values they carried, including the Protestant work
> ethic, belief in a Lockean individualism, distrust of concentrated

state authority, and other values. What I said at the time in defense of continued immigration into the United States, however, was that these cultural values had become deracinated from their particular ethnic roots and had become a possession of all Americans. But the cultural proclivity still matters.[9]

So maybe they are not that far apart as the debates during the 1990s seemed to imply.

Notes

1. See Harrison and Huntington, *Culture Matters*.
2. Fukuyama, "'End of History' 20 Years Later."
3. Fukuyama, "Clash at 25."
4. Rubenstein, "Francis Fukuyama on Identity Politics and Diversity."
5. Fukuyama, *End of History*, 217.
6. Rubenstein, "Francis Fukuyama on Identity Politics and Diversity."
7. Rawls, *Political Liberalism*.
8. "Democracy and Its Discontents."
9. Fukuyama, "Clash at 25."

SEVENTEEN

How Can We Make Liberal Democracies Thrive?

The nation-state is not obsolete; on the contrary, it has become more important. The balance between nationalism and international cooperation is hard to strike. Many issues have international solutions, but they need nations to cooperate. Fukuyama believes in the nation-state as the largest political unit and believes we need to allow irrational feelings to play a role when we identify ourselves with our nation.

Basing National Identity on Democratic Values

There is an important distinction between nation and state. You have said that "state building ultimately has to rest on a foundation of nation building."[1] What is nation-building? How can the state contribute to nation-building?

The state consists of the formal institutions, the government, the legal system, and the constitutional order. The nation is a more informal set of shared narratives and values that make people feel they are living in the same society and believe in the legitimacy of the same fundamental institutions. The two are quite different. It's much easier to build a state than it is to build a nation. The nation can be affected by the state through the educational system and through what leaders say and in the stories that people tell about themselves, but you can't just pass a law and create a nation.

What is a nation?

This is one of the questions to which modern democratic political theory does not provide us with a good answer. Many of the nations we have today were created in predemocratic times, and many are the product of considerable violence and force. Building nations is pretty difficult to do democratically.

This thin line between an aggressive and a benign nationalism is not an easy balance. How do you sort the elements?

This is a problem in Europe, not so much with Norway but with Germany and Italy, in the countries that have this history of fascism, because in the past their nationalism degenerated into fascist nationalism. It's a mistake because you can't have a democracy without a sense of national identity. It's just that national identity has to be built around democratic values and not around ethnicity or religion.

In *The End of History* you write about nationalism and liberalism. Can you explain how the relationship between them developed historically?

Liberalism came first, but they developed together. Since power is organized on a national basis, it is important to have a unifying national identity. They've always existed in a kind of uneasy tension, and one of the big problems is that the nation-building part is much easier to do under an authoritarian regime than under a liberal democracy because you can impose rules, and you can force people to live a certain way over extended periods of time. All modern democracies are the lucky inheritors of nations that were formed by nondemocratic means, and their stability is due to the fact that they simply inherited these nations, but they didn't have to create them.

In the current political climate, nationalism has again surfaced. How do you see this development? Is this nationalism that you believe in?

You need a national identity that's based on democratic values, meaning that it has to be open, tolerant, and accessible to everybody that lives in a country as a citizen of the nation. One big problem in Europe is that many people, especially on the Left, cannot accept the idea that you can have this kind of common democratic national identity. They associate anything with the word "nation" in it with the old-fashioned aggressive, intolerant nationalism of the early twentieth century. That's a big mistake because you can't have a democracy unless you have a sense of national identity, meaning the common belief in the legitimacy of your own democratic institutions and values. The attachment needs to be emotional and not simply intellectual, because if it's just intellectual, you could decide "Well, okay, I don't like my country that much."

What about the right wing's claim to nationalism?

Well, a lot of these right-wing parties are saying we ought to go backward toward a kind of ethnic understanding of the nation. A man I met in the Netherlands complained about Muslims having more babies and that this development would overwhelm the native Dutch. My answer to that was that, as long as he has an ethnic understanding of what it means to be Dutch, no outsider could ever become Dutch, so the understanding of what being Dutch means has to change.

You've described the idea of creedal identity. What do you mean by this? How do we go about creating one?

The sense of national or creedal identity is basically a matter of narratives in every society. You grow up with certain stories about who you are, where you came from as a people, traditions, things that you celebrate in common. That's the way you establish that emotional connection. I have an example from the film *Invictus*, which was about the 1996 rugby World Cup in South Africa. Nelson Mandela deliberately tried to get Black South Africans to support the almost all white rugby team, the Springboks. Because that's where you generate emotion. Most people don't care about abstract things like rule of law. They do care about sports. The reason that he was a great visionary leader was that he saw that you couldn't create this multiracial society if the different racial communities had different sports heroes. Mandela wanted to create a national team that everybody would support, and that's the function of leadership.

You also work in developing countries and countries with weaker states. Can foreigners help build supportive institutions, or does it have to be the citizens themselves?

It's not the case that foreigners have never built institutions in other countries. A lot of modern Indian institutions came from Britain, but the British were there for two hundred years, and it took a long time.

The reason foreigners have a hard time building states is that state building will not be successful if there is no parallel effort at nation-building in the sense of developing the set of narratives and symbols that make people think they're part of the same polity. That is something that foreigners really are not able to do. It has to come from within a society because only the people that live there know about their own traditions and history and so forth. They can make up stories that will be effective, and the most effective state builders are the ones that paid a lot of attention to creating those narratives. So, for example, in Japan at the time of the Meiji Restoration, the Meiji state builders deliberately used Shinto as a unifying ideology. Shinto had existed for centuries in Japanese culture. Shinto was also connected to the role that they saw for the emperor, which was as a unifying symbol of the country. They basically pushed this religious agenda. No outsider could have done something like that.

To conclude about identity, is it the case that you don't like the concept of identity? How is it that identity affects politics and takes over from economic considerations?

Yes, right, I have nothing against identity. It's such a fundamental concept to the way that modern people think about themselves that it's not like you can get away from it. It just has to be the right kind of identity, and some of these partial identities that are based on race or ethnicity or nation can be very grossly misused—nationalism being the clearest example of that—but others are very important. But if you don't have a set of narratives and understandings about what you hold in common with your fellow citizens, you're not going to be able to interact with them. You're not going to communicate and make decisions. It's not identity per se. You need the right kind of identity, which I think in a modern democracy has to be nonracial, nonreligious, nonethnic, and built around political principles.

Finally, is the nation-state the "highest" possible level, or is it possible to think of liberal democracy in a wider sense? And even if it is possible, is it normatively desirable to have liberal democracy beyond the state?

It actually has a lot to do with the fundamental concept of democratic sovereignty. In both Britain and the United States, there's a current of thought that we know how to create a legitimate democratic community within a single nation, but we don't know how to do that internationally. International organizations are not nearly as democratic as individual nations are. If you cede too much authority to an international organization—particularly to one like the United Nations that is composed of a lot of countries that are not democratic—it's not clear how those decisions are going to be democratically legitimate, which is a reasonable criticism.

Creating a Pan-European Democratic Identity

This brings us over to the European Union. Is the European Union an "answer to Europe," making it possible to solve problems together and create better European societies, or is the European Union an obstacle to such a process? How do you see the European Union and the way forward?

Europe has survived two large crises over the euro and Brexit. In a certain way, Europe has gotten stronger because I think the British example is not one that has created a lot of imitators. Right now it's facing an even larger challenge in the form of COVID-19. The problem right now is that Europe hasn't really solved some of the underlying problems that led to these crises. It doesn't have a strong decision-making apparatus in fiscal and foreign policy, and yet it seems very strong in certain areas to ordinary citizens in a way that annoys them in terms of its overregulation of economic activity. These are all issues that I think need to be sorted out, particularly the basic question of the direction of Europe as a whole. The French are trying to take the reins in that struggle, but whether they'll succeed is not clear yet.

Do you have examples of struggles that need to be solved?

The European Union, as a political unit, has got some very deep problems. Its problem is weak institutions. Europe is really stuck right now because it's gotten to the point where it needs to complete a unification process if it's going to solve problems like a fiscal union, but politically that's really not possible. The euro, in my view, was a big mistake. While the 2010 euro crisis didn't lead to a collapse of the currency, it could recur at any point—and may, this time over Italy rather than Greece. The Schengen system also does not work, because Europe doesn't have secure outer borders. That's going to come back to haunt Europe. There's a lull in migration right now, but a lot of people from sub-Saharan Africa and the Middle East are going to want to move to Europe unless they secure that border, and that is just not politically tenable. It's more a failure of German leadership than anything else, which would be the subject of a much longer discussion. But it's also not possible to go backward. What is likely to happen is that people just muddle along, not going either backward or forward.

We can all probably agree that monetary issues have been very difficult because of the different economic situations in various countries, but there are other aspects of European unity that could be important, such as Europe as a peace project. Do you believe in those?

Yes, that original function is still an important one. No individual European country could ever aspire to affect the global balance as much as a unified Europe.

Is a federal Europe possible?

The hope is that you could have a gradual democratization of European institutions as well as a greater consciousness of a shared European identity that will not be imposed from the top. Hopefully, that may come up from the bottom over time. The European Union was based on an aspiration to create a postnational consciousness where everyone would see themselves as Europeans rather than Norwegians or Germans or French or whatever. It would have been nice if that had happened, but it hasn't. The nation-state remains the fundamental unit because that's where people's emotional loyalties reside and where political power resides. If you want to move to a more centralized Europe that is able to act like a single state, you need to create a pan-European democratic identity. But Europe is very far from that. The COVID-19 crisis has revealed that the same divisions between northern and southern Europe that were evident during the euro crisis are still there and that a new division between western and eastern Europe has opened up and is getting wider.

As long as the European Union does not have military power or power to defend its borders, it will not be federal?

It depends on what you mean by federal. By an American definition, Europe is already federal, if that means power residing in individual member states. If by federal you mean having a strong central authority, then Europe is very far from that and not likely to arrive there any time soon. Every member state has its own army and police, which alone can exercise coercive power. There's no European army and no European police. The European Union has created some centralized functions in the economic realm, but important powers related to foreign policy, fiscal policy, and citizenship remain tied to member states.

How do you think the political architecture of the European Union has been able to respond to, say, the migrant crisis?

Very poorly, and that's why the crisis triggered all of these populist protests, because the basic defect in the design of the European Union with regard to migration is that it has no way of defending its external borders. And if you have a system of free movement within Europe, but no way of securing those outer borders, then the whole system ceases to work. This, of course, has come back big time in the COVID-19 crisis, where the first instinct of many countries was to shut down their borders.

If you found yourself in the shoes of an EU commissioner, what would you do?

I, actually, in contrast to many Americans, think that the European Commission is doing God's work in many areas, particularly in the area of competition policy. They've done some extremely important work in trying to rein in some of these big technology companies, and that is something American authorities haven't done.

The most important changes are beyond the authority of the EU Commission and have to do with the structure of the union itself. The strongest parts of the European Union's structure are the least democratic. The basic problem with the European Union is that it's strong in all the wrong places. It's strong in economic regulation in ways that annoy people in terms of their food labeling and so forth, but it's very weak in important areas like foreign policy, where basically any one of the members can veto a collective action. The European Union can't criticize China, for example, because Hungary has a Chinese road project that they don't want to jeopardize. Now the Commission itself can't do anything about this. It's got a fairly limited field of activity, and what this requires is a kind of restructuring of power within the European Union, for instance, that the parliament has been getting more power over time. It is the most legitimate body within the European Union, and in the long run if you don't have that kind of a democratizing shift toward more legitimate parts of the European Union, it's going to be hard for that organization to exercise its powers properly.

Solving the Climate Crisis through International Cooperation

As if the challenges to liberal democracy are not enough, we have an over-riding climate challenge. When I met you in Oslo in February 2020, climate was much more visible in the political debate than last time we met early in 2019. What are your thoughts on the climate challenge in this altogether more troublesome global political situation?

There's much more consensus on this issue in Europe than in the United States. Unfortunately, American climate policy has fallen victim to our underlying polarization. To me, it is an unbelievable situation where people do not agree about the basic facts about global warming, and we have a substantial part of the Republican Party that believes neither that global warming is happening nor that it's caused by human activity, and therefore there's no reason to take action on it. This is one of the things that can in part be blamed on the internet. If you are a smart person searching for reasons not to believe in global warming, you go on the internet and you'll find thousands of sites that will fortify you in that belief.

While Europeans berate themselves for not doing more on the climate front, they're actually among the best global performers in terms of policy reform. The problem is that they're not all that important in terms of global climate. In the next twenty years, the largest emitters of carbon by far will be developing countries, especially China and India.

Climate change will obviously need a high level of international cooperation. Can you comment?

When you get to the specific problem of climate, I would refer you to a book written by Scott Barrett, a former colleague of mine who now teaches at the Earth Institute at Columbia. He wrote a book called *Why Cooperate?*, and he gives several examples of problems that need collective solutions internationally. The first one is an asteroid hurtling through space on a collision course with Earth that can wipe out humanity; the second is global disease prevention; and the last one is action on carbon emissions. He uses game theory quite elegantly to illustrate that some of these problems are relatively easily solvable and others are extremely difficult. The asteroid problem turns out to be the simplest to solve. It's a problem that really requires only the decisions by one country, if we have the technological means to throw the asteroid off its track. The United States or possibly China or Russia could just do this unilaterally without the need for international agreement.

Climate, on the other hand, is a wickedly tough problem because it requires large up-front investments of resources, and the benefits will flow to people in other countries or else will not appear until years in the future, long past the current election cycle. That's one of the reasons it's been very hard to mobilize stronger action in favor of doing things that are necessary. I don't see that short of a really catastrophic set of events that action on climate is going to happen.

Maybe an overreaching international agreement on carbon pricing will be difficult, but are there other ways of reducing the emissions of carbon?

I have one example because a colleague from Stanford who is very often in India and Bangladesh told me about it. They use a certain kind of charcoal-fired brick kiln that produces huge amounts of carbon. All across South Asia mud bricks are the primary building material. If you wish to cut the amount of carbon emissions, you could do so by two-thirds by switching to gas kilns. The one statistic that stuck in my mind from this study was that all of these brick kilns across South Asia emit as much carbon every year as all of the fossil fuel–powered vehicles in North America. Rather than worrying about emissions standards in rich countries, it might make sense to invest in kiln conversion in South Asia because the technology is there. But it means that rich countries are going to have to pay for a lot of these machines in poor countries, which politically is very hard to pull off.

Some people are saying that we need to stop growth and to abolish capitalism in order to come to a zero-emission society.

The problem is not capitalism, and there's no alternative form of economic organization that would deal with this problem better. A couple of years ago I had a debate with a professor at the University of Oslo who was arguing that China was a much better country in terms of dealing with climate issues. There's a lot of admiration among people that live in democratic countries for this kind of a strong authoritarian country that can make big decisions. However, it's pretty clear that China's record of carbon emissions is really not all that admirable. It surpassed the United States a few years ago in terms of the absolute volume of emissions. The Belt and Road Initiative, which is China's single biggest development plan, involves the projected investment of something like $2 trillion in new infrastructure in developing countries, and it has a big energy component to it. And about 90 percent of that energy component is based on fossil fuels. The Chinese are going to be building lots of coal-fired power plants. In fact, part of what they're trying to do is to move those power plants away from their own cities and move them to Central Asia.

What about economic growth?

The importance of growth for actually maintaining democracy in the contemporary world is important. If you do not have growth, then the only way that you can get richer is by predation, by taking resources away from somebody else in a zero-sum game. If you look at what life was like in the preindustrial world, it was basically an environment where the vast majority of the population were living just a little bit over the level necessary for survival. There were periodic famines, and the way that anyone could grow richer under those circumstances is by grabbing resources from somebody else. The idea that you would return to an extremely low-growth world is going to have a pretty disastrous effect. The issue is really not capitalism and growth itself.

Notes

1. Fukuyama, *State-Building*, 99.

EIGHTEEN

The Future of History

One of Fukuyama's important contributions to political theory—especially to democratic theory—is that he makes a two-step move. He criticizes the old, liberal contract theories and replaces them with his own sociobiologically anchored framework. His approach is based on a theory of human nature, rooted in recent advances in anthropology, and it posits that human collaboration is based on two basic principles: on kin selection and on reciprocal altruism. These two principles occur spontaneously whenever humans interact, as when trust and collaboration take place among family members and among interdependent friends. In this sense these principles are "natural" principles of interaction. They are also inconsistent with the requirements of a modern state, where favoring friends and family is usually referred to as "corruption" and seen as ruinous to impersonal government. The implication of this theory is important. To establish a modern state, the old "natural" principles of social association must be broken, and an impersonal, "unnatural" way to administer a state must be established. If the norm of impersonality is not observed, and bureaucratic procedures are not continuously enforced, the modern state will be repatrimonialized and will slide into corruption and decay.

American and European Liberal Traditions

Helena Rosenblatt has written a book called *The Lost History of Liberalism* that explains very well the contradictions between liberalism and democracy and the tensions that existed for almost a century after the French Revolution. She also gives an account of various liberal traditions in different countries. Her claim is that Americans understand liberalism as rights and that they have "forgotten" about obligations and the common good, elements vital to the thinkers she discusses, such as Benjamin Constant and Germaine de Staël.

Rosenblatt writes, "Historically, most liberals were moralists at heart. Their liberalism had nothing to do with the atomistic individualism we hear of today. They never spoke about rights without stressing duties. Most liberals believed people had rights because they had duties, and most were deeply interested in questions of social justice."[1] Mutual helpfulness was the key to civilization. It was the moral duty of free people to behave in a liberal way toward each other. And being liberal meant "giving and receiving" in a way that contributed to the common good.

How do you see these various liberal traditions?

In the United States you've had two competing traditions. One is usually referred to as a republican tradition. The other one is a more Lockean liberal one. In the republican tradition, liberty is conceived of as active self-government, meaning that to be free is to participate in your own self-government by being a citizen, not just by voting but by being in the army and taking part in debates and shaping policy and this sort of thing. J.G.A. Pocock has argued that the republican tradition starts with Machiavelli in his *Discourses*, where he praised the Roman republic for creating this kind of active citizenship, and that tradition was carried on into the new world.[2]

You find some early American authors who conceived of the American republic in these Roman terms. It's not just about the government leaving you alone but about people actively participating. When Alexis de Tocqueville talks about liberty, that's what he means, the ability of people to govern themselves without having to defer to the authority of someone higher. The trouble in the United States is that there has been what you might distinguish as a Lockean or (in a more extreme form) libertarian tradition that simply sees the state as a kind of necessary evil. Lipset argued that this really came out of the American founding where it was a revolt against the authority of the British monarchy and Parliament, and it was built around this distrust of the state per se.[3] That led to the second understanding of liberty, which is simply freedom from state authority.

Do you think this latter tradition is prevalent now?

This is the way contemporary Republicans now think about liberty: the only thing that can threaten liberty is the government. Private corporations or social pressure, they don't care about that. What they care about is the government, and that's the only source of tyranny in the world. Therefore, they want to weaken the government and to take away its resource base by not paying taxes and so forth.

I think this understanding of liberty is wrong because, in fact, you need a state, you need government, and that state is properly the locus of citizenship. In the libertarian tradition, all you have are rights. You have no duties. The state just has to make sure that you are able to live your individual life. It can't tell you how to live it. It has no authority over your final ends and so forth. These two traditions have coexisted in the United States. In Europe, the republican side is probably more pronounced.

Rosenblatt argues that the state is important in liberal thought. She is explaining the differences between the United Kingdom and Germany, saying that there is a liberal tradition in Germany as well, and actually that the German liberal tradition from the last century enhances the role of the state, whereas the Anglo-American tradition holds the view that the state must not be too dominant.

There's another liberal tradition in which liberty is rooted in law, and this belief is that law is the foundation of liberty because the law is what prevents the abuse of power. The law is what regulates power and prevents kings or executive authorities from being abusive and harming the rights of their citizens. This is yet another understanding of liberty that has a very deep European tradition. One thing I argued in my political order book is that Europe was unusual because law preceded all other institutions. There is law in Europe before there is a modern state, and there is certainly law long before there was democracy. That, I think, was an important advantage that Europe had, because it's very hard to develop this kind of rule of law once you get democracy.

The question of the functioning of the state has become more acute after the COVID-19 pandemic. You wrote quite early after the outbreak an article called "The Thing That Determines a Country's Resistance to the Coronavirus." What determines it?

The best-performing states in this crisis are those that have, first, good state capacity, meaning the public health infrastructure, people, and facilities to deal with mass sickness, and, second, widespread trust in the country's leadership. That trust is built partly on state capacity but also on the citizens' sense that the leadership is honest and seeking some kind of greater public interest. Trust is something more than legitimacy; a government can be legitimate but not trusted. Trust really has to do with competence and purpose.

We talked about neoliberalism. What is the difference from classical liberalism?

Neoliberalism was kind of an American invention because Americans have a political culture that is very anti-statist, and most classical liberals just never believed that. They always understood that states were necessary to provide institutional foundation for property rights for individual freedom and the like. We're now seeing an adjustment, but that's a rejection of neoliberalism and not the older liberal tradition.

I am a Norwegian and consider myself to be liberal in a European sense. Are you a classical liberal yourself?

That's a difficult question. I have definitely moved further to the left. At the present moment, my preferences are fairly conservative in the cultural realm, but they have moved fairly far to the left in economic policy because I think inequality has become a problem in a way that it wasn't thirty years ago. Liberal doesn't mean that you can do whatever you like; you also have a responsibility, and that responsibility part is often forgotten in neoliberalism.

Having a Modern State Will Always Be an Uphill Battle

In a premodern state, political power was built on a network of families and of relations that had mutual interests and was built in an environment where resources could be exchanged for political loyalty.

In a modern state based on the rule of law, bureaucrats and politicians are chosen independently of family relations or close personal connections, and their exercise of power is constrained and cannot be influenced by offering particular advantages to anyone in a governmental or elected position.

Is a modern state an uphill battle since we are always inclined to naturally choose family or relations?

Yes, that's basically the argument I made in *Political Order and Political Decay*. In some sense, having a modern state is not a natural situation. If you have a prolonged period of peace and prosperity where your elites are getting richer, they're going to use their power to try to corrupt the system, and I think that's been happening in recent years.

You sum this up in the last paragraphs of *The End of History*, using Nietzsche and his claim that "men without chests" describe the modern world and that modernity would be a "very sad time," in which the heroic exertions made on the road to attaining liberal democracy would give way to "the endless solving of technical problems, environmental concerns, and the satisfaction of sophisticated consumer demands."[4] Is this the way we are going?

Well, we should look at what that passage describes. It sums up a good deal of what preoccupies people these days. They feel the absence of big horizons and the possibility of more dramatic kinds of changes. This discourages people. It is also a strange thing because we have kind of reached what we wanted, but then it's not enough.

Do you still think the end of history makes people lazy or even unconcerned, or does it make one want to do something more because that is a basic human desire? Do you believe that we are witnessing a lack of enthusiasm for liberal democracies?

After several decades of relative peace and prosperity, many people now take liberal democracy for granted. They want substantive equality, better social outcomes, or recognition of themselves and the struggles of their particular group. The old elites, represented by the traditional center-left and center-right parties, have made a lot of compromises to stay in power and do not seem to be offering up real choices to many voters. It's striking how in Eastern Europe—in Poland, for example—the great majority of citizens have now had no conscious experience of living under communism and therefore no instinctive antipathy to authoritarian government.

On the other hand, the rise of a populist right has reminded other people of the value of some of their basic institutions. The system of checks and balances in the United States was something that many people took for granted, up until the time that Trump started to seriously challenge principles like the independence of the judiciary and congressional oversight.

Does apathy make us unwilling to stand up for liberal democracy?

It depends on who the "us" is that you are referring to. If "us" constitutes the United States today under the Trump administration, the problem is not apathy but a deliberate turning away from democracy. This is the first administration in a hundred years not to have paid at least lip service to the value of democracy globally. The United States today is not criticizing but, rather, is often praising authoritarian leaders like Orbán or Fattah el-Sisi, who have been readily violating liberal principles. Now, under conditions of the pandemic, we are too preoccupied with our own survival to pay attention to erosions of democracy in other countries.

If the "us" refers to the old established centrist parties and voters, then, yes, there was a degree of apathy in not taking the rising populist threat seriously at first. However, it could be that the pandemic has been good for liberals and bad for populists. The poll ratings of leaders like Angela Merkel and Jacinda Ardern have gone up as a result of their good performance, and bad leaders like Trump, Bolsonaro, and Lopez Obrador have seen setbacks. This may change as the economic recession drags on, but for now there is hope.

Some people are advocating for epistocracy—power being exercised by the knowledgeable. It may seem an alluring idea, but the road to technocracy is short, something that provides efficiency but not respect. What do you think about epistocracy?

All governments need technocratic advice, but they should never let technocrats rule. Technocrats see the world with certain embedded assumptions that can often be very wrong. Many of the technocrats managing the US and European economies in the 1990s and early 2000s accepted an overly simple view of the benefits of globalization and failed to appreciate the social and political consequences of opening up their economies to Chinese competition. They failed to see how the bank deregulation of this period would destabilize financial markets. And they failed to see how labor mobility within Europe, as well as a Schengen system that failed to secure Europe's outer borders, could be politically destabilizing and lead to a huge backlash movement.

On the other hand, replacing technocrats with a bunch of political cronies whose major qualification is their loyalty to the ruling party or president is also a road to disaster. Trump has been hollowing out the American bureaucracy by replacing career experts with inexperienced loyalists. Michael Lewis's *Fifth Risk* describes in painful detail how any number of highly accomplished civil servants across the US government were succeeded by total incompetents or not replaced at all due to a lack of respect for what the government does. After his acquittal in the impeachment process, Trump has gone on to purge all of the career officials who testified honestly about his dealings with Ukraine. Something similar has happened in Hungary and Poland, where the ruling parties have totally politicized their bureaucracies and judiciaries.

Ukraine—A Beacon of Hope

You have visited Ukraine many times, and you are hosting a program for promoting democracy there. How is it going? And why do you think it's important to be doing the work that you're doing in Ukraine?

Ukraine is a big, important country that has been trying to free itself of the Russian mixture of kleptocracy and authoritarian government. It's made a great deal of progress since 2014, which many people don't recognize. Ukraine is the single most important frontline state in the war against authoritarian expansion. If Ukraine doesn't succeed in preserving its independence and democracy and in dealing with its own corruption problem, then no other countries in the post-Soviet space will succeed either. That's why I've spent a lot of time in Ukraine in the last few years.

At the present moment, things are not looking so good there. In 2019 Ukraine elected a new president, Volodymyr Zelensky, and a new Parliament in which 70 percent of the members have never served in politics before, many of them young people. It looked like they were sweeping out the entire old political elite. But in 2020 it has become evident that Ukraine's oligarchs retain much of their power and continue to shape policy behind the scenes.

My theory of change is to sponsor leadership programs where we teach a lot of young Ukrainians about how democratic government is supposed to work and how they can help bring about policy reform. Whatever the larger political picture there, I can tell you that I come back optimistic every time I go to Ukraine. I work in these leadership programs where we teach a lot of young Ukrainians. There are a lot of younger people, in their thirties and forties. They didn't grow up under the Soviet Union, and they really want Ukraine to be a European country.

The Russians don't like this Ukrainian struggle for freedom and democracy?

The Russians have grabbed Crimea and the Donbas. They're doing everything they can to destabilize Ukrainian democracy. The problem goes even deeper: Putin doesn't believe that Ukraine has a right to exist as a separate country.

I think the annexation of Crimea and the invasion of the Donbas, while a terrible breach of international norms, was paradoxically good for the Ukrainian national identity.

I do think that it's the Ukrainian people who ultimately will solve this problem, and I have some confidence that over time this is actually going to happen.

The Spirit of 1989

We are coming to an end of a long conversation about liberal democracies. Do you believe the spirit of 1989 is out there?

Yes, I would point out that the world may not be as gloomy, because I do think that the spirit of 1989, this revolt against dictatorship, is still alive in the world today, and we've seen civil society pushing back against dictatorship in many countries just in the last few years. People are protesting in Ukraine, in Georgia, in Armenia, in Ethiopia, in Sudan, and in Algeria. The opposition to the Maduro regime in Venezuela is yet another example as well as the moving away from military rule in Burma. It's still the case that people do not like to live under authoritarian governments. The problem that they've had is the transition out of dictatorship. Oftentimes there's not a consensus on what sort of government is supposed to follow from a clearly disliked authoritarian state, and there's a failure to meet the challenges of democratic governance. That transition has been the real sticking point for many of these countries dealing with issues of endemic corruption. But the spirit, I think, is still there.

But voting in free and fair elections will still be the first step?

It depends on the country. In dictatorships, it often requires a popular mobilization to get masses of people into the streets to demonstrate against the regime's legitimacy. Getting to an initial election is a first step, but as we've seen in very many countries, there is a long sequence of institutions that need to be built to translate election results into a lasting democracy. And that democracy can always regress.

If you are lucky enough to live in a democracy, then the way to beat back populism and all these antidemocratic forces is to win elections. I'm often asked how is it that we're going to prevent the rise of populism in other countries, and there's a very simple answer: you vote. Political power still resides in the hands of people who vote in our democracies, and it really depends on the ability to mobilize people who want to support a liberal and open democratic order, to get them out to the polls to support parties, and to have leaders that are capable of articulating to the people why it's important to have this kind of liberal democracy. That means mobilizing especially young people, who tend not to vote in the same numbers as older people. It means thinking through policies and then listening to opponents, because sometimes they're right about certain things. If you simply regard your opponents as racists and xenophobic, you may not pick up some of the signals about things that are legitimately making ordinary people unhappy.

It is pretty clear that you don't like leaders like Donald Trump. Can you name one that you could admire, who has the right combination of appealing to people and who would preserve liberal order?

I think unfortunately that I have to say I couldn't think of any because, unfortunately, it's much easier to be a demagogue. It's much easier to play on people's fears, to stir up these kinds of emotions that are based on injustice that are felt by people that are searching for community and identity, and it's harder to find politicians that actually want to unify people in a democratic community that is diverse and respectful of other points of view. But I am still hopeful, and that's the task that remains for the next thirty years of human history.

Before we end, what are the main elements of your rethinking the end of history through the thirty years that have passed?

Politically, for me, the early 2000s saw two really big failures. One was the Iraq War and the other was the financial crisis, the global financial crisis, both of which were the products of certain conservative ideas, which forced me to rethink the logic of those underlying ideas. Also, the growth of inequality in that period became a much more evident problem by the time you got to the second decade of the twentieth century.

That accounts for the shift in my political position, but the other part of it is studying developing countries and institutions. In *The End of History*, the importance of a modern state didn't really register much. I didn't talk about that in that book. The need for a modern state is much clearer to me now. The whole idea of political decay was not in the original book, *The End of History*, and that now seems to me a really big problem in the United States and in Europe.

With the dramatic rise of inequality over the past three decades— inequalities that have been starkly underscored in the current pandemic—I don't see how you can fail to support policies that would provide better social protections for ordinary people. I don't think that my assumptions on this score have changed; the world has changed. But there are also big areas of continuity over thirty years. As you know, I raised the identity issue in *The End of History and the Last Man*, and this theme been there right from the beginning.

Notes

1. Rosenblatt, *Lost History of Liberalism*, 4.
2. Pocock, *Machiavellian Moment*.
3. Lipset, *American Exceptionalism*.
4. Fukuyama, *End of History*, 301.

Epilogue

When I started writing this book, I thought the spirit of 1989 was challenged by Trump and populism, but then came March 2020 and COVID-19, which soon spread around the globe. I am quite sure we will look back on 2020 as a pivotal year—but I am not sure if we have an optimistic decade ahead of us.

To me, the worst that could happen is not a disagreement on how liberal democracies work but that there would be no debates, criticism, and defense of liberal democracy when politics is turning more authoritarian, populist, and unfree.

This is what I believe we must keep an eye on: the capacity of bureaucracy and state institutions to solve the tasks they are set to do. Next, we must make sure that we have conflict-solving institutions and practices. We must maintain the open, participating, transparent, and liberal aspects of our societies—everyone must be included and respected. Democracy is the only political system that has the ability to learn, the only system where opposing and different interests can be heard. In democracies, it is possible to negotiate, arguments can be taken into account, and minorities can have influence or at least can be safeguarded. Liberal democracies ensure freedom and diversity. Thirty years ago, Fukuyama wrote the following: "For democracy to work, however, citizens of democratic states must forget the instrumental roots of their values and develop a certain irrational thymotic pride in their political system and a way of life."[1] If there is one thing to remember from all his writings, it must be the following: we must safeguard and defend liberal democracy so that the next decades turn out better for all.

—Mathilde Fasting, Oslo, Norway, December 31, 2020

Notes

1. Fukuyama, *End of History*, 215.

Acknowledgments

First of all, I wish to thank Francis Fukuyama for spending many hours talking to me and for accepting my suggestion to come to Stanford for the first important session of talks. It has been a privilege to become acquainted with Frank, as he is known among his friends, and to follow up our talks during his stay in Oslo in February 2020, just before the world was hit by COVID-19 and all travel was banned. I must also thank him for contributing in the editing process with valuable comments and clarifications.

Second, I must express my gratitude to Georgetown University Press and especially to the director, Al Bertrand. His comments and suggestions have been encouraging, and his support throughout the editing process has been particularly valuable, making sure that the manuscript became both timeless and relevant. The editing process took place during the first phase of the pandemic of COVID-19 when both Norway and the United States were in lockdown. I must admit that incorporating the pandemic into the manuscript has been challenging, but I hope the result is acceptable. It was hard to predict the fall of the Berlin Wall but maybe even harder to foresee that this pandemic would paralyze the world.

This project started out as a small book in Norwegian, based on a version of my original Norwegian manuscript and the Stanford interviews in 2019. I wish to thank the Norwegian editor of that book, Edvard Thorup at Dreyer, for encouraging me to contact Fukuyama for those interviews. I owe a special thanks to Jeff Gedmin, editor in chief and chief executive of *American Purpose*, for letting me use the title of the commemorating interview thirty years after the fall of the wall, "The Future of History," and for his belief in this project.

A special thanks to Frank's good friend Professor Dan Banik, who invited me to a private lecture and small dinner in Oslo in February 2018 with Fukuyama and also to different venues during Fukuyama's stay in Oslo in 2020, and to Ole Egil Andreassen for ideas, support, and valuable contacts. I wish to thank Hallvard Sandven for his careful reading of my interview guide and later drafts of this book. Torbjørn Lindstrøm Knutsen gave me valuable comments and support, and Helena Rosenblatt commented on the text and inspired me to focus on classical liberalism. I also wish to thank Branko Milanović, who reminded me that the end of the Cold War was not a time of happiness in his native country, Serbia and Yugoslavia, and took the time to explain and elaborate his views on economic history and institutions.

Finally, my daughter, Agnes; my son, Peder; and my husband, Lars have supported me all the time—thank you.

Literature

Fukuyama's bibliography is extensive and impossible to fully cover in a book such as this. The following bibliography gives a full overview of the literature, but here I give a rough outline of Fukuyama's main body of work.

After the publication of *The End of History and the Last Man* in 1992, Fukuyama wrote several books. Two interesting works from the late 1990s investigate the interaction of society and capitalism. The first is *Trust: The Social Virtues and the Creation of Prosperity*, published in 1995, which explored the social conditions of well-functioning economic systems. *Trust* narrates the history of economic growth, highlighting Adam Smith's thought not so much from *Wealth of Nations* but from *The Theory of Moral Sentiments*. Fukuyama's book is thus not only about technological and economic progress but also about ideas and values. The second is *The Great Disruption: Human Nature and the Reconstitution of Social Order* (1999), which tells the story of modernization and urbanization. Here Fukuyama investigates large-scale changes in norms, culture, and social relations in modern societies. *Our Posthuman Future: Consequences of the Biotechnology Revolution* followed in 2002, continuing his analysis of human nature in light of developments in biotechnology.

After this Fukuyama turned toward the structural conditions for democracy, state capacity, and state building, starting with *State-Building: Governance and World Order in the 21st Century* in 2004. The quality and the capacity of states and state bureaucracy have become more important to Fukuyama over the years. Two years later came *America at the Crossroads: Democracy, Power, and the Neoconservative Legacy*, which represented a parting from his previous political convictions. It was necessary for him to explain the faults of American foreign policy, especially in Iraq. In 2010 he published *Falling Behind: Explaining the Development Gap between Latin America and the United States*. He had turned his attention to Latin American countries and was studying their political shortcomings and analyzing the reasons for their differences with the United States.

The year after, in 2011, the first volume of his work on political order, *The Origins of Political Order: From Prehuman Times to the French Revolution*, was published; and three years later *Political Order and Political Decay: From the Industrial Revolution to the Globalization of Democracy* appeared. These two books cover the political systems of the most powerful countries in the world, explaining their differences, origins, and development. His latest book, *Identity: The Demand for Dignity and the Politics of Resentment*, came in 2018. Here, Fukuyama goes back to the thesis from *The End of History* about recognition and develops it further to explain current political developments. Together with *The End of History*, these three latest books contain Fukuyama's main ideas.

Books by Francis Fukuyama

America at the Crossroads: Democracy, Power, and the Neoconservative Legacy. New Haven, CT: Yale University Press, 2006.

The End of History and the Last Man, with a new afterword. 20th anniversary ed. New York: Penguin Books, 2012.

Falling Behind: Explaining the Development Gap between Latin America and the United States. Oxford: Oxford University Press, 2010.

The Great Disruption: Human Nature and the Reconstitution of Social Order. London: Profile, 1999.

Identity: The Demand for Dignity and the Politics of Resentment. New York: Farrar, Straus and Giroux, 2018.

Nation-Building: Beyond Afghanistan and Iraq. Edited by Francis Fukuyama. Baltimore: Johns Hopkins University Press, 2006.

The Origins of Political Order: From Prehuman Times to the French Revolution. New York: Farrar, Straus and Giroux, 2011.

Our Posthuman Future: Consequences of the Biotechnology Revolution. New York: Farrar, Straus and Giroux, 2002.

Political Order and Political Decay: From the Industrial Revolution to the

Globalization of Democracy. New York: Farrar, Straus and Giroux, 2014.

Poverty, Inequality, and Democracy. Edited by Francis Fukuyama, Larry Diamond, and Marc F. Plattner. Baltimore: Johns Hopkins University Press, 2012.

State-Building: Governance and World Order in the 21st Century. Ithaca, NY: Cornell University Press, 2004.

Trust: The Social Virtues and the Creation of Prosperity. New York: First Free Press, 1995.

Articles and Chapters by Francis Fukuyama

"Acemoglu and Robinson on Why Nations Fail." *American Interest*, March 26, 2012. https://www.the-american-interest.com/2012/03 /26/acemoglu-and-robinson-on-why-nations-fail/.

"Against Identity Politics: The New Tribalism and the Crisis of Democracy." *Foreign Affairs*, September/October 2018. https://www .foreignaffairs.com/articles/americas/2018-08-14/against-identity -politics-tribalism-francis-fukuyama.

"America: The Failed State." *Prospect Magazine*, December 13, 2016. https://www.prospectmagazine.co.uk/magazine/america-the-failed -state-donald-trump.

"America in Decay: The Sources of Political Dysfunction." *Foreign Affairs*, September/October 2014. https://www.foreignaffairs.com /articles/united-states/2014-08-18/america-decay.

"American Political Decay or Renewal: The Meaning of the 2016 Election." *Foreign Affairs*, July/August 2016. https://www.foreign affairs.com/articles/united-states/2016-06-13/american-political -decay-or-renewal.

"Capitalism & Democracy: The Missing Link." *Journal of Democracy* 3, no. 3 (July 1992): 100–110.

"China and East Asian Democracy." *Journal of Democracy* 23, no. 1 (January 2012): 14–26.

"Civil Society and Political Society." In *Jean Bethke Elshtain: Politics, Ethics, and Society*. Edited by Debra Erikson and Michael Le Chevallier, 317–31. Notre Dame, IN: University of Notre Dame Press, 2018.

"The Clash at 25: Huntington's Legacy." *American Interest*, August 27, 2018. https://www.the-american-interest.com/2018/08/27/huntingtons-legacy/.

"The End of History?" *National Interest*, no. 16 (Summer 1989): 3–18.

"The Future of History: Can Liberal Democracies Survive the Decline of the Middle Class?" *Foreign Affairs* 91, no. 1 (January/February 2012).

"The Heart of Populism Is Identity, Not Race." *Spectator*, October 17, 2018. https://spectator.us/populism-identity/.

"Identity and the End of History." *American Interest*, August 23, 2018. https://www.the-american-interest.com/2018/08/23/identity-and-the-end-of-history/.

"Identity, Immigration, and Democracy." *Journal of Democracy* 17, no. 2 (April 2006): 1–17.

"Identity Politics." Lecture, University of Oslo, Oslo, February 13, 2018.

"Identity Politics: The Demand for Dignity and the Nation State's Future." Lecture, Vienna, March 3, 2019.

"Is There a Proper Sequence in Democratic Transitions?" *Current History* 110 (November 2011): 309–10.

"Liberal Democracy as a Global Phenomenon." *Political Science and Politics* 24, no. 4 (December 1991): 659–64.

"Liberalism versus State–Building." *Journal of Democracy* 18, no. 3 (July 2007): 10–13.

Nafisi, Azar, and Francis Fukuyama. "Totalitarianism as a Mindset Can Be Anywhere." *American Interest*, March 22, 2020, https://www.the-american-interest.com/2020/03/22/totalitarianism-as-a-mindset-can-be-anywhere/.

"The Pandemic and Political Order." *Foreign Affairs*, July/August, 2020, https://www.foreignaffairs.com/articles/world/2020-06-09/pandemic-and-political-order.

"Political Consequences of the Protestant Reformation." Parts 1–3, *American Interest*, October 31, 2017; November 2, 2017; and November 11, 2017.

"Reflections on *The End of History* Five Years Later." *History and Theory* 34, no. 2 (May 1995): 27–43.

"Reflections on *The End of History*, Five Years On." In *World History:*

Ideologies, Structures, and Identities, edited by Philip Pomper, Richard Elphick, and Richard T. Vann, 199–216. Malden, MA: Wiley, 1998.

Schulz, William, Robin Fox, and Francis Fukuyama. "The Ground and Nature of Human Rights." *National Interest*, no. 68 (Summer 2002). https://nationalinterest.org/article/the-ground-and-nature -of-human-rights-another-round-1156.

"Second Thoughts: The End of History 10 Years Later." *NPQ* 16, no. 4 (Fall 1999): 40–42. https://doi.org/10.1111/j.1540-5842.1999 .tb00074.x.

"Seymour Martin Lipset 1922–2006." *American Interest*, August 1, 2007. https://www.the-american-interest.com/2007/01/08/seymour -martin-lipset-1922-2006/.

"Social Capital and Civil Society." *IMF Working Paper* 2000, no. 74 (March 2000).

"Social Capital and the Global Economy: A Redrawn Map of the World." *Foreign Affairs*, September/October 1995. https://www .foreignaffairs.com/articles/1995-09-01/social-capital-and-global -economy-redrawn-map-world.

"States and Democracy." *Journal of Democratization* 21, no. 7 (August 2014): 1326–40.

"Statsviternes superstjerne Francis Fukuyama." *Aftenposten*, October 7, 2015. https://www.aftenposten.no/norge/i/4d1nl9/Video-fra -Aftenposten?video=102081.

"The Thing That Determines a Country's Resistance to the Coronavirus." *Atlantic*, March 30, 2020. https://www.theatlantic.com /ideas/archive/2020/03/thing-determines-how-well-countries -respond-coronavirus/609025/?utm_campaign=the-atlantic&utm _content=edit-promo&utm_term=2020-03-30T10%3A30%3A38 &utm_source=twitter&utm_medium=social.

"30 Years of World Politics: What Has Changed?" *Journal of Democracy* 31, no. 1 (January 2020): 11–21.

"Transitions to the Rule of Law." *Journal of Democracy* 21, no. 1 (January 2010): 33–44.

"Trump and American Political Decay." *Foreign Affairs*, November 9, 2016.

"US against the World? Trump's America and the New Global Order." *Financial Times*, November 11, 2016.

"The US vs the Rest." *NPQ* 19, no. 4 (Fall 2002): 8–24. https://doi
.org/10.1111/j.1540-5842.2002.tb00096.x.

"What Is Governance?" Center for Global Development, Working
paper 314 (January 2013).

"What Is Populism?" *American Interest*, November 28, 2017.

"What Would a Second Trump Term Do to the Federal Bureaucracy?"
Washington Monthly, April/May/June 2020. https://washington
monthly.com/magazine/april-may-june-2020/what-would-a-second
-trump-term-do-to-the-federal-bureaucracy/.

"Why Is Democracy Performing So Poorly?" *Journal of Democracy* 26,
no. 1 (January 2015): 11–20.

"Why National Identity Matters." *Journal of Democracy* 29, no. 4
(October 2018): 5–15.

"Why Populism: The Populist Surge." *American Interest*, February 9,
2018.

"Why Populist Nationalism Now?" *American Interest*, November 30,
2017.

Interviews with Francis Fukuyama

"The Beginning of a New History." Interview by Jacques Attali. *NPQ*
31, no. 1 (January 2014): 20–24. https://doi.org/10.1111/npqu.11421.

"The Challenge of Positive Freedom." Interview by Nathan Gardels.
NPQ 24, no. 2 (Spring 2007): 53–56. https://doi.org/10.1111/j
.1540-5842.2007.00885.x.

"The China Model: A Dialogue between Francis Fukuyama and
Zhang Weiwei." *NPQ* 28, no. 4 (Fall 2011): 40–67. https://doi.org
/10.1111/j.1540-5842.2011.01287.x.

"Democracy and Its Discontents." Interview by Wesley Yang. *Esquire*,
October 17, 2018. https://www.esquire.com/news–politics
/a23695274/francis-fukuyama-trump-democracy/.

"Donald Trump and the Return of Class." Interview by Natalia
Koulinka. *Opendemocracy*, January 20, 2017.

"The Economist Asks: Francis Fukuyama." Interview by Anne McElvoy.
Economist Radio, September 13, 2018. Podcast, 18:32. https://
soundcloud.com/theeconomist/the-economist-asks-francis.

"The 'End of History' 20 Years Later." Dialogue with Kishore Mah-

bubani. *NPQ* 27, no. 1 (Winter 2010): 7–10. https://doi.org/10
.1111/j.1540-5842.2010.01124.x.

"The End of the International Liberal Order?" *Stanford CDDRL*,
May 10, 2017. YouTube, 1:17:47. https://www.youtube.com/watch
?v=scAzukYHJjY&utm_content=buffer44ffb&utm_medium=
social&utm_source=facebook.com&utm_campaign=buffer&fbclid
=IwAR0HPlOAk5i-B20b0vebckSQHf06YPh9pJ6bErO56RqDalu
3J3mqIMU4nAo.

"Filosof: Vi glemmer, at ideer er magt." Interview by Anders Ellebæk
Madsen. *Kristeligt Dagblad*, May 13, 2017. https://www.kristeligt
-dagblad.dk/kultur/filosof-vi-glemmer-ideer-er-magt.

"Fiscal Crisis Erodes EU Legitimacy." Interview by Michael Skafidas.
NPQ 28, no. 3 (Summer 2011): 68–73. https://doi.org/10.1111
/j.1540-5842.2011.01273.x.

"Francis Fukuyama." Interview by David Runciman. *Talking Politics*,
October 17, 2018. Podcast, 49:48. https://www.talkingpolitics
podcast.com/blog/2018/120-francis-fukuyama.

"Francis Fukuyama: Democracy Needs Elites." Interview by Alexander Görlach. *NPQ* 34, no. 2 (May 2017): 9–13. https://doi.org
/10.1111/npqu.12075.

"Francis Fukuyama: Democracy still rules. But will US catch up in a
changing world?" Interview by Michael Skafidas. *Christian Science
Monitor*, June 8, 2011. https://www.csmonitor.com/Commentary
/Global-Viewpoint/2011/0608/Francis-Fukuyama-Democracy-still
-rules.-But-will-US-catch-up-in-a-changing-world.

"Francis Fukuyama: 'If You Don't Have a Sense of National Identity, You Can't Have a Democracy.'" Interview by Vicent Partal.
VilaWeb, February 2, 2020. https://english.vilaweb.cat/noticies
/francis-fukuyama-if-you-dont-have-a-sense-of-national-identity
-you-cant-have-a-democracy/.

"Francis Fukuyama: Trump Instinctively Picks Racial Themes to
Drive People on the Left Crazy." Interview by Tim Adams. *Guardian*, September 16, 2018. https://www.theguardian.com/books
/2018/sep/16/francis-fukuyama-interview-trump-picks-racial
-themes-to-drive-people-on-the-left-crazy.

"Francis Fukuyama om korona, Kina og Trump." Interview by
Mathilde Fasting. *Liberal halvtime*, July 7, 2020. Podcast, 40:28.

https://pod.space/liberalhalvtime/ep-137-francis-fukuyama-om
-korona-kina-og-trump.

"Francis Fukuyama on COVID-19." Interview by Yascha Mounk. *The Good Fight*, May 27, 2020. Podcast, 58:24. https://podcasts.apple
.com/us/podcast/francis-fukuyama-on-covid-19/id1198765424?i=
1000475923269.

"Francis Fukuyama on Democracy, Trump and the US Election."
Interview by Mathilde Fasting and Eirik Løkke. *Liberal halvtime*,
February 12, 2020. Podcast, 34:01. https://pod.space/liberalhalv
time/ep-110-francis-fukuyama-on-democracy-trump-and-the-us
-election.

"Francis Fukuyama on Identity Politics and Diversity." Interview
by Adam Rubenstein. *Weekly Standard*, October 9, 2018. https://
www.washingtonexaminer.com/weekly-standard/interview-francis
-fukuyama-on-identity-politics-and-diversity.

"Francis Fukuyama on the Fruits of Dignity Politics." Interview by
Tom Jacobs. *Pacific Standard*, October 10, 2018. https://psmag
.com/social-justice/francis-fukuyama-on-the-fruits-of-dignity
-politics.

"Francis Fukuyama Says Identity Politics Are Killing America and
Empowering Donald Trump." Interview by Nick Gillespiel. *Reason
.com*, September 26, 2018. Podcast, 56:10. https://soundcloud.com
/reasonmag/francis-fukuyama-says-identity-politics-are-killing
-america-and-empowering-donald-trump.

"Francis Fukuyama, senk farten på inntaket av flyktninger." Interview
by Thea Storøy Elnan. *Aftenposten*, October 7, 2015. https://www
.aftenposten.no/kultur/i/KG77/Francis-Fukuyama-Senk-farten-pa
-inntaket-av-flyktninger.

"Fukuyama: Donald distrugge tutto Ma gli europei non devono mol-
lare." Interview by Antonello Guerrera, *La Repubblica*, May 29,
2017. https://ricerca.repubblica.it/repubblica/archivio/repubblica
/2017/05/29/fukuyama-donald-distrugge-tutto-ma-gli-europei-non
-devono-mollare06.html?ref=search.

"Fukuyama: Populismen peger paa ægte problemer, man har forkerte svar." Interview by Esben Schjørring. *Altinget*, April 6, 2019.
https://www.altinget.dk/artikel/184485-fukuyama-populismen
-peger-paa-aegte-problemer-men-har-forkerte-svar.

"Fukuyama: Vesten er traadt inn i en helt ny politisk epoke. Og det er forfærdeligt." Interview by Adrian Joachim. *Information*, September 19, 2016. https://www.information.dk/kultur/2016/09 /fukuyama-vesten-traadt-helt-ny-politisk-epoke-forfaerdeligt.

"History's Pallbearer." Interview by Nicholas Wroe. *Guardian*, May 11, 2002. https://www.theguardian.com/books/2002/may/11 /academicexperts.artsandhumanities?CMP=share_btn_link.

"Identity and Its Discontents." Interview by Richard Aldous. *American Interest*, September 19, 2018. Podcast, 29:12. https://www.the -american-interest.com/podcast/episode-202-identity-and-its -discontents/.

"Identity Politics." Interview with Francis Fukuyama, Josie Rourke, Roseanne Chantiluke, and Eric Kafumann, by Andrew Marr. *BBC Radio 4, Start the Week*, October 15, 2018. Podcast, 42:00. https://www.bbc.co.uk/programmes/m0000qtr.

"Is America Ready for a Post-American World?" *NPQ* 25, no. 4 (Fall 2008): 42–46. https://doi.org/10.1111/j.1540-5842.2008.01022.x.

"The Last Man and the Future of History." Interview by Charles Davidson and Jeff Gedmin. *The American Interest*, May 3, 2019. https://www.the-american-interest.com/2019/05/03/the-last-man -and-the-future-of-history/.

"The Man Who Declared the 'End of History' Fears for Democracy's Future." Interview by Ishaan Tharoor. *Washington Post*, February 9, 2017.

"Mini-Trumps Are Coming All over Europe." Interview by Jens Münchrath and Anke Rezmer. *Handelsblatt*, December 29, 2017. https://www.handelsblatt.com/today/politics/francis-fukuyama -mini-trumps-are-coming-up-all-over-europe/23573578.html.

"Modi Is Pretty Impressive, Says Francis Fukuyama." Interview by Tunku Varadarajan. *Open*, May 26, 2018. http://www.openthe magazine.com/article/cover-story/modi-is-pretty-impressive-says -francis-fukuyama.

"On Why Liberal Democracy Is in Trouble." Interview by Steve Inskeep. *NPR*, April 4, 2017. https://www.npr.org/2017/04/04 /522554630/francis-fukuyama-on-why-liberal-democracy-is -in-trouble?t=1595770603615.

"Protectionism against China Is No Answer to America's Woes." *NPQ* 27, no. 3 (Summer 2010): 28–31. https://doi.org/10.1111/j .1540-5842.2010.01178.x.

"There Are No Shortcuts to 'the End of History.'" Interview by Nathan Gardels, *NPQ* 23, no. 2 (Spring 2006): 34–38. https://doi.org/10.1111/j.1540-5842.2006.00804.x.

"Trump è il president più ignorante. Anche per colpa della Silicon Valley." Interview by Massimo Gaggi. *Corriere della sera*, May 3, 2017. https://www.corriere.it/esteri/17_maggio_17/fukuyama-trump-presidente-piu-ignorante-anche-colpa-silicon-valley-0b790e26-3a74-11e7-acbd-5fa0e1e5ad68.shtml.

"What Follows the End of History? Identity Politics." Interview by Evan Goldstein. *Chronicle of Higher Education*, August 27, 2018. https://www.chronicle.com/article/What-Follows-the-End-of/244369?cid=wcontentgrid_41_2.

Other Literature

Acemoglu, Daron, and James A. Robinson. *Why Nations Fail: The Origins of Power, Prosperity, and Poverty*. New York: Crown, 2012.

Barrett, Scott. *Why Cooperate? The Incentive to Supply Global Public Goods*. Oxford: Oxford University Press, 2007.

Coleman, James S. *Foundations of Social Theory*. Cambridge, MA: Belknap Press of Harvard University Press, 1990.

Collier, Paul. *Exodus: How Migration Is Changing Our World*. Oxford: Oxford University Press, 2013.

———. *The Future of Capitalism: Facing the New Anxieties*. London: Allen Lane, 2018.

Collier, Paul, and Alexander Betts. *Refuge: Rethinking Refugee Policy in a Changing World*. Oxford: Oxford University Press, 2017.

Creppell, Ingrid. *Toleration and Identity: Foundations in Early Modern Thought*. New York: Routledge, 2003.

Dalmia, Shika. "Where the West Went Wrong." *The Week*, October 9, 2018. http://theweek.com/articles/800359/where-west-went-wrong.

Diamond, Jared. *Guns, Germs and Steel*. New York: Norton, 1997.

Diamond, Larry. *Ill Winds: Saving Democracy from Russian Rage, Chinese Ambition, and American Complacency*. New York: Penguin, 2019.

Donnersmarck, Florian Henckel von. *The Lives of Others* [Das Leben der Anderen]. USA: Sony Pictures, 2007.

Engerman, Stanley L., Kenneth L. Sokoloff, Miguel Urquiola, and Daron Acemoglu. "Factor Endowments, Inequality, and Paths of Development among New World Economies." *Economia* 3, no. 1 (Fall 2002): 41–109.

Freedom House. "Freedom in the World 2019: Democracy in Retreat." https://freedomhouse.org/report/freedom-world/2019/democracy-retreat.

Friedman, Milton. "The Social Responsibility of Business Is to Increase Its Profits." *New York Times*, September 13, 1970.

Gardels, Nathan. "Francis Fukuyama: Identity Politics Is Undermining Democracy." *Washington Post*, September 18, 2018. https://www.washingtonpost.com/news/theworldpost/wp/2018/09/18/identity-politics/?utm_term=.f53988371638.

Giridharadas, Anand. "What Is Identity?" *New York Times*, August 27, 2018. https://www.nytimes.com/2018/08/27/books/review/francis-fukuyama-identity-kwame-anthony-appiah-the-lies-that-bind.html.

Habermas, Jürgen. *The Structural Transformation of the Public Sphere: An Inquiry into a Category of Bourgeois Society.* 1962. Reprint, Cambridge, MA: Polity, 1989.

Hamid, Shadi. "The End of the End of History." *Foreign Policy*, November 15, 2016.

Harrison, Lawrence E., and Samuel P. Huntington. *Culture Matters: How Values Shape Human Progress.* New York: Basic Books, 2000.

Hirschman, Albert O. *The Passions and the Interests: Political Arguments for Capitalism before Its Triumph.* Princeton, NJ: Princeton University Press, 1977.

Holmes, Stephen, and Ivan Krastev. *The Light That Failed: A Reckoning.* London: Penguin, 2019.

Huntington, Samuel P. *Political Order in Changing Societies.* New Haven, CT: Yale University Press, 1968.

———. *The Third Wave: Democratization in the Late Twentieth Century.* Norman: University of Oklahoma Press, 1991.

Klein, Ezra. "Francis Fukuyama's Case against Identity Politics." *The Ezra Klein Show* (podcast), September 27, 2018. https://www.youtube.com/watch?v=F7D_mF_siSk.

Krastev, Ivan. *After Europe.* Philadelphia: University of Pennsylvania Press, 2017.

Levitsky, Steven, and Daniel Ziblatt. *How Democracies Die: What History Reveals about Our Future*. New York: Crown, 2018.

Lipset, Seymour Martin. *American Exceptionalism: A Double-Edged Sword*. New York: W. W. Norton, 1995.

Marshall, Alfred. *Principles of Economics*. London: Macmillan, 1890.

Marx, Karl, and Friedrich Engels. *The German Ideology*, Parts 1 & 2. 1846. Reprint, Mansfield, CT: Martino, 2011.

Mason, Paul. *Postcapitalism: A Guide to Our Future*. London: Allen Lane, 2015.

McCloskey, Deirdre Nansen. *Bourgeois Dignity: Why Economics Can't Explain the Modern World*. Chicago: University of Chicago Press, 2010.

———. *Bourgeois Equality: How Ideas, Not Capital or Institutions, Enriched the World*. Chicago: University of Chicago Press, 2016.

———. *Bourgeois Ethics: Ethics for an Age of Commerce*. Chicago: University of Chicago Press, 2006.

———. *How to Be Human—Though an Economist*. Ann Arbor: University of Michigan Press, 2000.

———. *Why Liberalism Works: How True Liberal Values Produce a Freer, More Equal, Prosperous World for All*. New Haven, CT: Yale University Press, 2019.

Menand, Louis. "Francis Fukuyama Postpones the End of History." *New Yorker*, September 3, 2018.

Milanović, Branko. *Capitalism Alone: The Future of the System That Rules the World*. Boston: Harvard University Press, 2019.

———. "Francis Fukuyama against Mainstream Economics." *global-inequality* (blog), March 29, 2019. http://glineq.blogspot.com/2019/03/francis-fukuyama-against-mainstream.html.

———. "A Grand Fresco: The Origins of Political Order." *global-inequality* (blog), March 25, 2019. http://glineq.blogspot.com/2019/03/a-grand-fresco-origins-of-political.html.

Mounk, Yascha, "The End of History Revisited." *Journal of Democracy* 31, no. 1 (January 2020): 25–35.

North, Douglass. *Institutions, Institutional Change and Economic Performance*. New York: Cambridge University Press, 1990.

North, Douglass C., John Joseph Wallis, and Barry R. Weingast. *Violence and Social Orders: A Conceptual Framework for Interpreting*

Recorded Human History. New York: Cambridge University Press, 2009.

North, Douglass C., and Barry R. Weingast. "Constitutions and Commitment: The Evolution of Institutions Governing Public Choice in Seventeenth-C." *Journal of Economic History* 49, no. 4 (December 1989): 803–32.

Olson, Mancur. *The Logic of Collective Action: Public Goods and the Theory of Groups*. Boston: Harvard University Press, 1965.

Philippon, Thomas. *The Great Reversal: How America Gave Up on Free Markets*. Boston: Harvard University Press, 2019.

Piketty, Thomas. "Brahmin Left vs Merchant Right: Rising Inequality & the Changing Structure of Political Conflict (Evidence from France, Britain and the US, 1948–2017." World Inequality Database, Working paper, no. 7 (2018): 1–180. http://piketty.pse.ens.fr /files/Piketty2018.pdf.

Pocock, J.G.A. *The Machiavellian Moment*. Princeton, NJ: Princeton University Press, 1975.

Pritchett, Lant, and Michael Woolcock. "Solutions When the Solution Is the Problem: Arraying the Disarraying in Development." Working paper No. 10 (Washington, DC, Centre for Global Development, 2002). https://www.cgdev.org/publication/solutions-when -solution-problem-arraying-disarray-development-working-paper-10.

Przeworski, Adam, and Fernando Limongi. "Modernization: Theories and Facts." *World Politics*, 49, no. 2 (January 1997): 155–83.

Putnam, Robert. *Bowling Alone: The Collapse and Revival of American Community*. New York: Simon and Schuster, 2000.

Rawls, John. *Political Liberalism*. New York: Columbia University Press, 1993.

Rosenblatt, Helena. *The Lost History of Liberalism: From Ancient Rome to the Twenty-First Century*. Princeton, NJ: Princeton University Press, 2018.

Runciman, David. "Fukuyama on History." *Talking Politics–History of Ideas*, May 25, 2020. Podcast, 47:00. https://soundcloud.com /kuhakumarx/fukuyama-on-history.

———. *How Democracy Ends*. London: Profile Books, 2018.

Sachs, Jeffrey. *The End of Poverty: Economic Possibilities for Our Time*. New York: Penguin, 2005.

Sagar, Paul. "The Last Hollow Laugh." *Aeon*, March 21, 2017. https://aeon.co/essays/was-francis-fukuyama-the-first-man-to -see-trump-coming.

Sloterdijk, Peter. *Rage and Time: A Psychopolitical Investigation.* New York: Columbia University Press, 2010.

Smith, Adam. *The Theory of Moral Sentiments.* Indianapolis: Liberty Classics, 1982.

Stitt, Ross. "The Rise of the Ungovernable." *Quilette*, March 1, 2019.

Tilly, Charles. *Coercion, Capital, and European States.* Cambridge, MA: Blackwell, 1990.

Tooze, Adam. "Democracy and Its Discontents." *New York Review of Books*, May 2019. https://www.nybooks.com/articles/2019/06/06 /democracy-and-its-discontents/.

Williams, Howard, David Sullivan, and Gwynn Matthews. *Francis Fukuyama and the End of History.* Cardiff: University of Wales Press, 1997.

Withers, Matt. "Francis Fukuyama and Kwame Anthony Appiah Take on Identity Politics." *The Economist*, August 25, 2018. https://www.economist.com/books-and-arts/2018/08/23/francis -fukuyama-and-kwame-anthony-appiah-take-on-identity-politics.

Yang, Chan-young. "Revisiting Fukuyama: The End of History and the Clash of Civilizations, and the Age of Empire." PhD thesis, Wesleyan University, Middletown, Connecticut, April 2010.

Zakaria, Fareed. "I Wanted to Understand Europe's Populism. So I Talked to Bono." *Washington Post*, September 20, 2018.

Index